THIS
IS IT

Maple Spring Publishing Titles

THIS IS IT

FEATURES BONUS BOOK:
QUIET MOMENTS WITH GOD

JOSEPH MURPHY

MAPLE SPRING PUBLISHING

Published 2024 by Maple Spring Publishing

THIS IS IT. QUIET MOMENTS WITH GOD. Copyright © 2024 Maple Spring Publishing. All rights reserved.

Front cover design by David Rheinhardt of Pyrographx

Interior design by Meghan Day Healey of Story Horse, LLC.

Library of Congress Cataloging-in-Publication Data is available upon request

ISBN: 979-8-3505-0072-1

10 9 8 7 6 5 4 3 2 1

Contents

1

Divine Guidance

"If thou knewest the gift of God, and who it is that saith to thee, Give me to drink, thou wouldest have asked of him, and he would have given thee living water." —JOHN 4:10.

The living water means inspiration. The word inspiration comes from the Latin "Spiro," meaning I breathe into. We breathe air without effort, likewise we must let the Divine Light or creative essence of God flow through our intellect without tension. The subjective mind in us perceives by intuition. It does not have to reason or inquire as it is all-wise, infinite intelligence. If you say to your subconscious, sometimes referred to as the subjective mind (being subject to the conscious mind), "Wake me up at seven o'clock," you know that you awaken exactly at the time specified. It never fails.

We must realize that herein lies a source of power which is omnipotent. Many good people have erroneous ideas about being inspired. They believe that it is an extraordinary event to be experienced by mystics or highly spiritual people, and they think it applies to prayer and the Bible only. This is not true.

Any business man or woman may be inspired by turning to God, and information or divine guidance may be received for any problem. Your business problem can be solved by turning to God for the answer and your information may be general or specific. For example, if you are an executive of a commercial organization and you want a new idea for your sales program, try the following technique. If you are in business, have a private office where you will not be disturbed; close your eyes; be still; think of the attributes and qualities of God, which are within yourself. This will generate a mood of peace, power and confidence. Then speak in the following, simple manner to the Father within who doeth the works, "Father, thou knoweth all things, give me the idea necessary for a new program." Begin to imagine that you now have the answer and that it is flowing through you. You must not pretend; really believe it; accept it and then drop it. The latter is most important and is the secret of the whole process.

After the silence, get busy; do something; become preoccupied with routine matters. Above all do not sit around waiting for the answer. It comes when you think not and the moment you expect not. The inner voice of intuition speaks like a flash—it is always spontaneous and unannounced. You may get any type of information which will help you along the road to success.

Intuition, which means being taught from within, knows the answer and does not require previous experience. We must realize that God has no problems, if He had, who would solve them? Therefore, when we pray, we know that God has only the answer; He knows no problem, hence we rise to the point of recognition of the answer. The answer flows through the problem and there is no problem. No reasoning power is involved and the amazing suddenness with which the solution comes, sometimes is startling. In our Young Peoples' Forum we now teach intuition and inspiration; they find it fascinating and illuminating.

Intuition is the soft tread of the unseen guest. We must welcome this King of Kings and sing His praises; then He will make frequent visits. The abandonment of the intellectual reason for the wisdom of God is intuition. We abandon our objective reasoning only in the sense of deferring it to a higher guide. After we have received an intuition, we use reason in carrying it out. You may get specific information about anything.

For example, you may be writing a book and require special data, perhaps written 1000 B. C. The information may be in the British Museum or in the New York Public Library. It might take you days or weeks to find it, if you do not know specifically what you want. In such instances, relax; be still and say silently and quietly to your Father (your subconscious), "Thou knowest all things, give me this information." Drop off to sleep with the one word "answer." In that relaxed mood you repeat the word "answer."

Your subjective is all-wise; knows what type of answer you desire and will answer in a dream, as a hunch, or feeling that you are being led on the right track. You may get a sudden flash to go some place—a person may give you the answer. "I have ways that you know not of." Many are led to an old book store, where they pick up the very book that gives them the desired data. We must be ever watchful for impressions as Divine guidance, for when a feeling or idea comes to us, we must be able to recognize it.

There are two reasons why we may not acknowledge our hunches. These reasons are tension and failure to recognize them. If we are in a negative, despondent, bitter mood, Divine guidance is impossible. As a matter of fact only negative guidance will prevail. If we are in a happy, confident, joyous mood, we will recognize the flashes of intuition that come to us; moreover, we will feel under subjective compulsion to carry them out. It is necessary, therefore, to be still and relaxed when you pray for guidance; for nothing can be achieved by tenseness, fear or apprehension.

Who has not had the experience of being unable to remember a name, then dropping the search, have the name come to him later during repose? If you try too hard to hear a telephone ring, you cannot.

Let us consider the failure to recognize the voice of intuition. For example, suppose we are gazing idly into a store window. An eccentric millionaire puts a $500 bill in our hand. We throw it away thinking it is an advertisement for a dance hall or a beauty parlor. We must be on the alert for Divine ideas or feelings that come to us, and be able to recognize them. In emergencies guidance comes immediately, because we lean all our weight on the Christ within; thus we place all our burden on him and are free; then comes salvation. The answer to everything is within. "You would not have sought me, had you not already found me."

For business and professional people the cultivation of the intuitive faculty is of paramount importance. Intuition offers instantaneously that which the intellect or reasoning mind of man could accomplish only after weeks or months of monumental trial and error. When our reasoning faculties fail us in our perplexities, the intuitive faculty sings the silent song of triumph.

The conscious mind of man is reasoning, analytical and inquisitive; the subjective faculty of intuition is always spontaneous. It comes as a beacon to the conscious intellect. Many times it speaks as a warning against a proposed trip or plan of action. We must listen and learn to heed the voice of wisdom. It does not always speak to you when you wish it to do so, but only when you need it.

If we will only believe, and not pretend to believe, that God is guiding us now in all our ways, in all our thoughts, words and deeds, we shall be led along the right road. Artists, poets, writers and inventors listen to this voice of intuition. As a result they are able to astonish the world by the beauties and glories drawn from this storehouse of knowledge within themselves.

Become still, relax, close your eyes and say, "Father, thou knowest all things. I am writing a novel. Give me the characters, names, locations and setting." Rejoice that the answer is flowing through you now; drop off to sleep with the word "novel" on your lips, silently repeating it until you are lost in the deep of sleep. The word "novel" is etched in the subconscious. In the morning or a few days later, you will sit down to write; the words will flow; ideas will come in an unending stream and you will say, "Thank you, Father."

The word "intuition" also means "inner hearing." The oldest definition for "revelation" meant "that which is heard." Jesus said, "As I hear, I judge." Hearing is not the only way to nurture intuition. Sometimes it comes as a thought, but the most common way is to "hear the voice." Many times it is a voice whose texture, color and substance you can hear as plainly as the voice over the radio. The scientist uses his wonderful gift of imagination and in the silence he sees fulfillment. His intuition relates to his particular science.

Intuition goes much farther than reason. You discard reason; then comes intuition. You employ reason to carry out intuition. When you receive intuition, you will often find that it is opposite to what your reasoning would have told you.

This is how one young lady in the advertising business produces her wonderful slogans. She drops off to sleep with the word "slogan" on her lips, knowing that the answer will be forthcoming. It always is—"He never faileth."

2

Power To Choose

Theology has always accounted for the presence of evil in the world by the invention of a devil.

The inner meaning of the Old Testament clearly indicates that its writers did not believe in the devil. You are told—several times openly, and always secretly—that the Lord was responsible for evil as well as for good. The Lord, or law, referred to is the law laid down by man, because of his foolish beliefs in sickness, disease, fear, death, old age and all other ills. This is the law decreed by man, and is different from the laws of the Lord God. The laws of electricity, motion, physics and mathematics are example of these laws. We are learning the nature of these laws and specializing them in numerous ways. These laws are neither good nor bad—they are facts in nature.

In reading the Gospels the word *devil* is not found in the earlier versions. It is mentioned therein "as a spirit of evil." In the teaching of Jesus there is no mention of the theological devil. This was later invented by certain writers. Furthermore, let us realize that the word we have translated as "devil" is "a" spirit of evil, not "the" spirit of evil.

Thus Jesus taught that there were many spirits of evil. Constantly the narrative states that He went around expelling the devil from human beings. The spirits of evil spoken of are the moods of hate, jealousy, revenge, remorse and fear. The many phobias, fixations and other destructive negative thoughts which man is capable of conceiving are also spirits of evil.

Jesus is symbolized in the Scriptures as the great teacher of Truth. He explained the laws of life by recounting parables, allegories and fables to the multitude. "But without a parable spake he not unto them." He healed all men by seeing them as perfect as their Father in heaven. He proved to them that any man can overcome any obstacle—be it what it may—that besets his path. All that was necessary was for man to believe that the God within could do all things. Jesus' whole mission was to teach people how to find the Christ within, or the true self, which does all things in the name of the Father. In those days man thought that it was too good to be true. Today we still find millions believing in powers apart from themselves and living in dread of the unknown. Countless millions are victims of belief in war, crimes, disease and the power of environment and circumstances to hold them down.

It might be said that the devil is God upside down. The devil is God as He is misunderstood by the so-called wicked or ignorant. God is all, and all there is God. He is absolute, the only One, and everything is made inside and out of the Absolute. He has created all things and nothing exists apart from God. He is infinitely good and perfect and the author only of perfect good.

The devil is everything that God is not; therefore, the devil is not. The devil is wrong thinking and feeling; these powers result in wrong action or expression. Man having free will—that is, the freedom to choose happy or despondent moods—creates his own good and his own evil. He is not compelled to love, but he has freedom to love. Love is joyous and spontaneous and we have the freedom to give or retain it. God did create a being out of Himself but did not decree that he must love Him. No, that would not be love, because man would then be an automaton, and all of us would be truth students.

You will realize there would be no joy unless we knew the opposite. How could man know what joy is except he could experience the opposite? Man is conditioned into this world and becomes conscious of opposites—such as north and south, east and west, hot and cold, positive and negative, darkness and light, male and female, night and day, ebb and flow. These constitute man's evil or limitation. He finds that he has to travel from New York to Chicago due to his belief in travel. He will continue to do this until he awakens from his dream of limitation, and finds that all he has to do is to feel that he is in Chicago; really believe it, and he will be there; for Chicago is within himself. He does not go there—he brings "thereness" here. When we find God or the Oneness, all opposites or sense of duality disappear.

The first thing we must realize is that there is no power to challenge God for His throne. If this were true, God would not be God. He is omnipotent, omnipresent and all-wise. He is infinite intelligence. "Ye shall know the Truth and the Truth shall make you free." Understanding of Truth frees man from want, fear, sickness, all superstitions and false beliefs of the race. The devil has been created by people who were unable to account for the apparent evil in the world. They reasoned in this fashion: God was omnipotent, but was powerless about the devil.

If any man is now dwelling in hate, that is his personal devil and it will hurt him. If any man believes in external forces capable of injury or destruction, this man is really saying, "God is supreme, yet He is not supreme." He creates a devil who becomes His successful rival. God asks you to forgive your enemies; yet He cannot forgive His own; for he has created a place of everlasting punishment for them, even though admittedly He is all powerful; this of course is an absurd position.

From the foregoing analysis it might be said that the only evil is the belief in evil. All things and all activities are from One source—God. It must follow, therefore, that there can be nothing intrinsically evil. The evil comes from our incomplete state of consciousness—from our seeing things incorrectly. Reflect that what we call evil in humans we do not call evil in animals, but it is the conditioned responses to natural instincts. Our incomplete state of consciousness, our misapplication and our misapprehension of Universal laws constitute what the world calls evil. We insist upon doing things that will hurt us, even after we have discovered that they hurt us. We prefer the immediate gain though it blinds us to the consequent pain.

The hell spoken of by some is not the punishment dealt out by an angry God. It is the consequence of man's own acts, brought upon himself. He can free himself from this hell, when he is willing to take the necessary steps and undergo the self-discipline of right thinking, right feeling and right action.

What greater self-discipline is there than the constant application of the Golden Rule? "As you would that men should do unto you, do you also unto them in like manner!" Likewise, as you would that men should feel about you, feel you also about them in like manner. As long as man refuses to believe that God is good, there remains but one way out—the Via Dolorosa—undergoing pain and suffering.

The word that means "devil" in Hebrew is a word meaning "slanderer" or "a liar." The devil is one who tells lies about reality. A slanderer tells lies about man. The eye slanders a fact because it deals only with the outside appearance of fact. People say, "The sun rises and the sun sets," but it neither rises nor sets. We see nothing as it is in reality, because our eyes are geared to see according to our beliefs. If, for example, our eyes were geared in any other way, we would see things differently. We would see circumstances differently, and they could become something else in our sight.

According to the Ancient wisdom the word "mirth" is connected with the letters AYIN, which means the eye. The reason for this is that the surface appearance is different from the reality. AYIN is associated with what seems rather than what is—with illusion rather than reality; this is the most mirthful thing about the "devil." The real meaning of "devil" in the Hebrew language is the "slanderer"—one who tells lies about the Truth.

We might point out that as man awakens, he builds a finer and finer instrument until he no longer needs an instrument—he sees without eyes; then man sees reality, because the illusion of the thing does not stand in his way. With the mind's eye, he sees beyond the form to the reality behind. In other words, he sees divinity beyond the mask. Without eyes the spiritual man sees "Truth" everywhere. He knows that One and not two is the beginning and end of all. However, two—good and evil—are the aspects One presents to mankind, because men are subject to the illusion of duality.

Fools, deluded by outward appearance, create a demon out of the web of their folly. The awakening is that divine understanding which comes to a man who succeeds in meditation, and "the last day" is the time of that achievement. The wise man sees and knows that the demon is the shadow of the Lord. "Happy is the man that findeth wisdom, and the man that getteth understanding. For the merchandise of it is better than the merchandise of silver, and the gain thereof, than fine gold." (PROV. 3:13–14).

The belief that desire is a personal affair is due to a misunderstanding of the Divine urge present in all men. The urge towards growth which everyone feels, is not from the personality; nor can this urge be satisfied by accumulating things of the world. Man's desire for power, authority, possessions and fame are mistaken desires, *the reason being they are all for limited forms.* They set up the law of contraction instead of expansion. Let us have the desire of being rather than of having; then we will unite ourselves with a source of power that no degree of expression can diminish.

It is true, however, that our subjective mind fulfills or grants mistaken desires also, and this is often the cause for our bitter experiences. The desire to get things such as hats, automobiles, fur coats and houses is a disappointing one. When one gets what he desires in the material way, he must then desire something else, but in this way he does not grow spiritually. Eventually he must look for something which will not fade when he gets it. There is only one such desire—that is to give life, love, peace, wisdom and beauty to mankind. "I am come that you might have life and have it more abundantly." As with all other desires the more we get, the more we want.

We must remember, it is more blessed to give than to receive. We do this by seeing the "Untouchable glory of God" in others. The more we see It in others, the more It will shine out in ourselves. By doing this daily, we are preaching the Gospel or good news. The more we give in this manner, the more we have. The true gift is that which we give ourselves in consciousness by feeling the reality of the wonderful state we desire to see manifested in the other. To take our desires from the world of limitation—which is eating of "the fruit of the tree of knowledge of good and evil"—brings us disillusionment and pain. It is by these "stripes" we are healed—made whole in consciousness.

The innermost nature of Being is the tendency to give more life, therefore, all desires may be tested in this manner. Let man ask himself if the realization of his desire will enable him to give out more life, love and beauty to his world. If this is true, it is a desire that is never disappointing. "The more you give the more you have." On the lower scale we find that the more you get, the more you want.

There is an inexhaustible storehouse in man, from which he can draw forth security, peace and happiness—this is the Kingdom of Heaven spoken of in the Bible. Having found peace and happiness within, all other things are added to him. The only time is NOW. All experience is *now*. All Action is *now*. Let us experience the Kingdom of Heaven *now*, for God or our Good is the eternal *now*.

3

Rebirth

It is often asked, "Why do we have dictators, despots and tyrants in the world?" These are extensions in space of the dictator complex present in the hearts and minds of all human beings.

Instead of trying to force our opinions on others, we must learn how to change ourselves and we will change the world.

What is the world? The world is ourselves in aggregation. Napoleon still lives, Ghenghis Khan still lives, as do Caesar and all others. They live in the consciousness of the race. Our boys and girls learn about them at their mother's knees, at school and in college. They burn with resentment and rage at the apparent wrongs committed by these men. They read avidly of the crimes, atrocities, and acts of violence. These states are impressed on their subconscious minds. All of these moods, feelings and thoughts which are entertained become objectified as living realities. Moreover, these boys and girls suffer from nightmares, hysteria and various complexes because these moods of fear, hate, anger and resentment become the ghosts that walk the gloomy galleries of their minds.

Living in these states of mind—dwelling on dictators and tyrants, realizing that whatever is impressed in consciousness must be expressed in the world—man should not be surprised when these tyrants of the past are reborn into our society, because we actually call them forth. It is true in a sense, therefore, that Ghenghis Khan is reborn or reincarnated. He is an embodiment of the state of consciousness of the people, nation, race or world, whatever the case may be. The reader will see, that it is not a man who lived a thousand or two thousand years ago who is being reborn. It is a state of consciousness that is born again.

When a mother places a child on her knee; whispers in his ear that he is God walking the earth and tells him that he can do all that Jesus did, she is seeing her boy as God had planned. If the mother believes her statements, her belief will be automatically transferred to the child's subjective consciousness, and he will become her ideal. "I was young, now I am old, yet never have I seen the righteous forsaken nor their seed beg bread." If parents live the Law, if teachers teach the Law of life—the Truth of Being to the young; then their seed shall never beg bread. This means these children shall never become the beggars, outcasts, thieves and tyrants of the world. No, they shall fulfill the ideals of the parents. They must fulfill the prayer of the parents because true prayer is always answered.

If parents will impress their subjective minds with wonderful dreams for their boys or girls, then according to their *belief,* "will it be done unto them." By changing our opinions, beliefs, ideas and ideals by teaching the youth of the nation who they really are, by showing them the way, the truth and the light, we can build the Kingdom of Heaven on earth; then we will prevent the rebirth of dictators, despots—former undesirable states of consciousness— which are perpetuated by prejudices, racial hatreds and fear of the unknown.

Let us teach children of the great accomplishments of the poets, artists, engineers, chemists, physicists, astronomers and others. Let them emulate these great men. There is so much for a child to learn about the great writers of the world and the giants of world literature, that the beautiful works of man cannot be exhausted in what is ordinarily called "a lifetime." After he is taught good, the child will emulate good.

In reality we are all dreaming; when man fully awakens he knows that planets are thoughts, suns and moons are thoughts, and his own consciousness is the space which sustains them all. He begins to realize that the whole world is a thought. For example, he becomes aware of the fact that the body is not real, but it is a thought or idea held in consciousness. The body has no life apart from consciousness. He realizes that there is absolutely no reality to matter or the body of man; it is a group of ideas and opinions. Man gives life to ideas and opinions as long as he believes them. When he disbelieves the errors, these ideas have no life in them.

Man was never born and he will never die. There is no death. Death is an idea that exists in the minds of men. As long as man believes in death, he must witness and experience it. Man has no beginning and no end; he always was, just as God always was, is and shall be. "God and man are one." "I and my Father are one."

The man who is always quoting so-called authorities to prove the modern theories of reincarnation is himself without authority. He is still crying in the wilderness and calling other men masters and adepts. Call no man master. "Salute no man on the highway." Salute the God within. The Kingdom of God is within, and if someone tells you it is "Lo here; lo there," believe him not. The Kingdom of Heaven is within man.

Where is the Truth? *It is within yourself.* "Look within—search the Scriptures," said Jesus. This means that all has been written in your subjective mind "from the foundation." All knowledge is within; all wisdom is within; all beings that ever lived are within you *now*. You can project the likeness of any living being, past or present; for all men are states of consciousness—qualities of mind expressed. *All moods, tones, qualities and vibrations are within you, because God is within and He cannot be divided—all is contained in the part.* Christ cannot be divided, and Christ means consciousness. The subjective Self of man—the Christos or Christ-man, the so-called Jesus Christ or God-man knows all men are within himself. He knows that, objectively speaking, all beings are projections in space of himself—the One Man.

Are there not thousands of cases over the world of men who have completely lost their former identity and personality; assumed new lives; entered different professions, and in many cases even remarried? These men were victims of amnesia, or loss of memory concerning their former selves. They could not remember their former wives or children. They had no recollection of their former professions or occupations. They assumed a new role in life. They were changed men entirely, because they had changed their consciousness. There is only consciousness!

Let us stop quoting authorities on spiritual subjects. As long as we quote authorities, we cease to be THE authority. All power is given to us in Heaven and on earth. Let us use it. In the spiritual sense we are all victims of amnesia. We have forgotten who we *really* are, and we tell ourselves that we are worms of the dust.

Take, for example, a man who goes to sleep and when he awakens he has completely forgotten who he is, and gravitates to the slums. His social world becomes the slums. His friends, knowing what has happened, try to coax him back to his former status. Because of amnesia his former way of life is entirely blotted from his memory. He believes his place is in the slums; he only smiles at these old acquaintances whom he no longer knows. He accepts as true the role he now plays.

The day comes when his memory is restored and he awakens to his rightful status. With certainty and promptness he returns to the environment consonant with the dignity of his upbringing. He wonders why he is in the slums. What has transpired is all a dream, a dream of the unreality. "Awake thou that sleepest, and arise from the dead, and Christ shall give thee light." (EPH. 5:14). Let us awake to the Real and return to our Father's house. "Everyone that thirsteth, come ye to the waters, and he that hath no money; come ye, buy, and eat; yea, come, buy wine and milk without money and without price." (IS. 55:1)

Man does not have to become a victim of amnesia in order to change his consciousness. He can read the 10th Chapter of Samuel, book 1, and learn how he can be turned into another man. This is accomplished through prayer. Take the story of the boy born of lowly parents, in a manger, having all the handicaps socially and financially that any child could have at that period in history. It was said, "Can there anything good come out of Nazareth?" (ST. JOHN 1:46). The word "Nazareth" symbolizes to sprout or grow, and man should be ever watchful not to despise the day of small beginnings.

This boy Jesus walked the earth and imagined himself to be the perfect man, capable of seeing only perfection in everything. He felt the reality of the wish within him and it became a conviction. Having imagined the state he wished, and having felt the reality of the state imagined, all the necessary qualities for the fulfillment of that state came from within himself. They were always there, but they had to be recognized before they became manifest in the world of man. This boy did as Samuel said man should do, which was, "Go up into the Hill of God—thou shalt meet a company of prophets coming down from the high place playing music, and thou shalt prophesy with them,—and shalt be turned into another man." (SAMUEL 10:5)

The Hill is a high state of consciousness; the other prophets represent the eternal trinity employed in the creation of all things—consciousness, idea and the joyous feeling or conviction that it is done. *The "feeling" is the conviction that unites consciousness desiring with the thing desired.* The joy of answered prayer is the music of the three prophets. It is the inner silent knowing of the soul. Therefore, any man can turn his back completely on the past;—forget all the old beliefs and foolish ideas of the race mind; enter into the joyous thrill of being Jesus (saving consciousness) and do his work. If he remains faithful to this mood and sustains it, he will automatically develop all the qualities necessary to do "even greater work."

The story of Jesus is a portrayal of what all men should be. It is a complete refutation of all age-old beliefs regarding man's handicaps of race, national origin, environment and circumstance. All these things are as naught when man discovers who he really is; so let us keep our eyes on God. It is there, where man sees no obstacle. When he takes his eyes off God, or his good, he sees his limitations and obstacles. NOW is the day of salvation; let us see the light now; for God is the Eternal Now—since time is an illusion of the senses. The awakening takes place now.

We know that everything exists in the Infinite. There is nothing that any man can think of, no matter how fantastic, that does not already subsist in the Infinite. It may be said to exist when we acknowledge it or witness it. *Nothing is made; nothing becomes; all is and all is God.* We are wedded to the belief in time, so we conceive of ourselves conditioned by time. Yet the Bible tells us, "For a thousand years in thy sight are but as yesterday when it is past, and as a watch in the night." (PSALM 90:4).

If time is a belief, which it really is, the common belief of reincarnation cannot be true. The theory tastes good and looks good, but let our prayer be: "lead us not into temptation." God tempts no man, but our conscious mind and five senses are tempted to believe this false doctrine. It becomes a panacea assuaging our wounded pride or feeling of inferiority. Moreover, it causes us to turn back or tempts us to eat of it. "But in the day that thou eatest thereof thou shalt surely die," because we are eating of the fruit of the tree of knowledge of good and evil. This tree means world belief, power in other gods hence the breaking of the first Commandment, "Thou shalt have no other Gods before me."

We must eat of the tree in the midst of the garden, which is man's consciousness—God dwelling within him giving all power to Him. We "eat" of Him by taking part in a psychological feast of being a noble, dignified and Christ-like person. We must see the Christ in all men, sermons in stones and good in everything. When we do this, all other things shall be added unto us. Man's life on this plane is like the several stanzas of a poem or the scenes of a play, because it really is the One Being dramatizing Himself as the many. Common sense is the most uncommon sense, because it is God's or good sense. Wisdom or common sense teaches that illumination or the great awakening to our Godhead can happen here and now. "If it be not now, yet it will come; the readiness is all."

In order to elucidate this point, take a solid, metallic substance and heat it. The temperature rises, but for a while it looks as if no change were taking place. However, the moment that degree of heat is reached, which denotes its melting point, it begins to liquefy, thus changing its shape and seemingly its nature also. Likewise, water can be turned into steam which is invisible—pure steam cannot be seen. Water also becomes snow, ice and hail— all different rates of vibration of the one substance. When a liquid is changed into a gas, these changes are brought about by an increase in the rapidity of vibration of the constituent particles whether they are solid or liquid. The same applies to man. What is true on one plane is true on another, for God changes not. The rebirth comes to that man here and now—not in after life. There is no transforming power in death. Man raises his rate of vibration by lifting himself up to a high state of awareness, by entering into the thrill of being that which he longs to be, and by feeling the joy of accomplishment.

Man is a porous being, plastic and pliable, capable of being moulded into any state he can imagine. He is nothing but "liquid light." In the meditative mood he stills the mind, thereby immobilizing the senses by focusing his attention exclusively on the one ideal—only one. He suggests sleep to himself by feeling sleepy, being careful not to fall asleep, however; the mystic in meditation must always keep control. In this mood he knows, feels and sees himself as being bathed in a sea of liquid light. A flame or lights appear all around him and he knows that in this floating liquid state he can mould, fashion and shape all that he longs to be, to do and to possess.

In this state he contemplates the joy of the answered prayer. The feeling of accomplishment fills him, and he dwells on the reality of his desire for perhaps five minutes, two minutes or ten minutes. By constantly praying in this manner, there is an expansion of consciousness—it is like the heat that melts the solid. The day comes when man melts away all inhibitions, fears and doubts, and becomes the God man here and now. To such a man, physical laws and time disappear. This change may come in the twinkling of an eye like the volatilization of a liquid into a gas.

The reason the modern theory of reincarnation is popular is because man, using his five senses only, is like the five foolish virgins—he has no oil or wisdom in his lamps. He finds that this explanation gives him solace and tells him what he wants to hear. At the same time it seems to unfold many unexplained phenomena. Such acceptance retards spiritual progress, checks the awakening process and is a destructive, superstitious belief. The modern accepted belief in reincarnation is very old; as is the belief in purgatory, hell and the devil.

The Bible mentions reincarnation several times and some of these references are explained in this book. The Scripture informs us that Herod believed in reincarnation. Herod represents the world or the five-sense man, the man ignorant of spiritual laws who subscribes to tradition and family beliefs. A man who believes that John, Elias, or some prophet long since dead, is risen from the dead, is symbolized by Herod. What this type of man fails to see is that it is always God coming forth as a quality, tone, or mood of man himself.

Mozart, Bernini, Lincoln, Shakespeare, and Napoleon left their impressions with mankind. We read of their works in history, song and prose. All of them live in the hearts or subjective minds of man. A man's son is his idea or feeling about anything. He can give conception to any state he is capable of conceiving. If a man, therefore, admires and dwells on the qualities and attributes of Napoleon, and would love to give birth to such a son, "as within so without." During the creative act a Napoleon-like character appears resembling the mood of that man. In other words, it is the tone struck during conception or creation that determines the nature of the child.

The worldly-minded man called Herod in the Bible, believes in a physical reincarnation, and he desires to see Jesus, or the Truth as told in the ninth chapter of Luke. However, the Truth student will readily see that such a man cannot see him, "as no man hath seen the Father." The latter is always a subjective perception or feeling within man. Man awakens by degrees, slowly or quickly. On arising from bed in the morning, he rarely awakens all at once. It takes him a minute or so. The thermometer, however, does not skip any degrees. Before man fully awakens from his dream no necessary step in unfoldment will be omitted. All limitations and inhibitions will be dissolved.

The following article about the violinist Zimbalist appeared in "The New Yorker" some years ago: "Nobody told Zimbalist he was supposed to play the piano, too; during the final examinations in his eighteenth year, they handed him a Beethoven Sonata to be read at sight in the presence of the whole faculty. He had never touched a piano except to get his 'A.' He sat down, however, got his breath and played. When he finished he was told to close the book and repeat the whole Sonata from memory. He did so. After a moment of silence the room broke unanimously into applause—an unheard-of demonstration."

The man of the world would not conceive of this as being possible. The power within man is capable of setting at naught all human beliefs and man-made laws. We must begin to take our attention away from the limited, human concept of ourselves; then we shall, like Mozart, compose music at six, statues at seven, and at the age of twelve we will confound the wise men of the world. Many cases are reported where cripples invalided for years leap and run in the presence of fires. In emergencies mothers lift automobiles to extricate their children. Where is this power? It is within themselves. Fires and emergencies are not needed to stir the gift within. Man can do this in the quiet of his own soul. We create in "silence."

4

The Bible and Man

Man cannot interpret the Scriptures in their proper light until he is at a point of spiritual development comparable to the writers of the Bible. Man must get into the meditative mood. He must ask the All-Wise within himself what He, Himself, meant when He (consciousness) wrote that Bible passage thousands of years ago. The reader of this book must realize that he wrote the Bible but he has forgotten it. His subjective mind knows and remembers all. It knows the truth about reincarnation and all other so-called mysteries of life.

Dwelling on the past like Lot's wife, we are turned slowly but surely into a pillar of salt. In other words, we are preserving the past. We are wedded to it and are held in bondage to false beliefs or Karma (evil that has to be expiated here in life), and to many other strange and weird ideas. As long as man believes those things, he must suffer the consequences of his beliefs, ideas and opinions. Disease is ignorance, and the modern, accepted conception of reincarnation is similar to a disease. It is worse than the effects of opiates, alcohol, or hashish, because it paralyzes the mind and destroys the body.

The writer's experience with people who believe in these ideas is that they are nearly all sick. However, they have perfect alibis which act as anesthetics to dull their senses, and to render them both numb and dumb to the truth. The anesthetic they inhale is not ether but much worse, since the effects of the former wear off. Likewise, the opinions, beliefs and foolish race concepts continue in the minds of these well-meaning but misguided people.

One will tell you that the reason she is now a cripple suffering from rheumatoid arthritis which cannot be cured, is that it is a Karmic debt, which she must pay, for a sin or error committed in a former life. Man must see the foolishness of all this. It is a complete contradiction of all the teachings of the Bible, which portray that man is God, individualized—One with the Father. "When you have seen me you have seen the Father." "I and my Father are one." Yes, truly, when you look at any man, you see God.

The Truth is that when man discovers that he is God, and that his unmodified consciousness or awareness is the invisible creator of all things, he will learn to overcome all obstacles, such as disease, suffering and frustration. In overcoming these he will awaken to his true power and his divinity, because he seeks the aid of no man. He then goes forth and proves his Godhood.

Man is both unconditioned and conditioned. The life principle—subjective or subconscious of man—is the awareness of being, or unconditioned consciousness. Man expressed is conditioned consciousness—or God expressing Himself as man. Man becomes that which he believes himself to be. "Whom do men say that I, the son of man, am?" Will you the reader, give the same answer that the world does by saying: "Some say that thou art John the Baptist: some Elias; and others Jeremiah, or one of the prophets?" (ST. MATTHEW 16:14). That is the belief of the world.

Read these words again in the Bible, ponder on their meaning. It will then reveal itself to you and you will not have to ask anyone what it means. "Peter" in the Bible means your inner voice, the Rock of Truth, which cannot be moved or swayed by the opinions of the world. This inner quality of mind is an attribute of God expressed in man. It is the disciplined hearing of the Truth student which reveals that you are Christ, the son of the living God. Now Jesus said, "Flesh and blood hath not revealed it unto thee, but my Father which is in Heaven." (MATTHEW 16:18). Yes, it is true that flesh and blood will never tell us who we are. It can never reveal the story or truth of re-birth. The flesh and blood spoken of is the world and its opinions, race consciousness, traditional beliefs and the attitude such as, "the old religion is good enough for me." The old religion is not good enough for anyone who seeks the truth on these matters. Blood means life. You give life to your ideas and to the opinions and concepts of the world as long as you believe them. Jesus tells us that Heaven is within ourselves. The Voice speaks and tells man, as it did Simon Peter, "Thou art Christ, the son of the living God." (MATTHEW 16:16).

The son is the offspring of the Father and must be like the Father. Is he not the image and likeness of the Father? Man is God conceiving Himself to be man—then man appears. We are here to discover who we are, to awaken from the dream of limitation and ignorance and to prove ourselves to be God. When we discover who we are, we will express the will of God, which is life, beauty, peace and love.

In the seventeenth chapter of Matthew we read: "But I say unto you, Elias has come already and they know him not." Elias means my God Jehovah. It is always God being born. Man does not believe it—neither does he know it. He thinks it is another person being reborn. Man is trying to divide the One, and by so doing he limits the Holy One of Israel.

It is always Elias that is born in the world—the spirit of the one God. Let us awaken here from the dream of limitation and separation. There is no other place or planet for us to go. Man cannot go outside himself. I am you and you are I—for there is but One. The hero and the most degraded criminal are really I also. One Being, God, is incarnated in two and one-half billion persons called the "human race."

People have inverted and distorted the Truth for thousands of years, but that is no reason why man should continue to do so. There are still people living on this globe who believe the earth is flat and that the sun rises in the east. There are millions that subscribe to the belief in disease. Let not man be blinded by his former beliefs. Rather, let him open his mind to the Truth of life.

If he approaches the study of the Bible,—which is purely allegorical, figurative and psychological—, he must not approach it with a closed mind. If he does he will color it to meet his former opinions which are fixed within him. Such a man can never find the Truth. You cannot pick up anything if you are holding something in your two hands. If you hold fast to your former beliefs, you are turning back and limiting the Holy One of Israel. A closed mind is unable to grasp the Truth.

When man sheds the garment called the body, he continues to live subjectively in a dream state.

All the moods that he carried over with him into this present state are experienced in the form of a dream. Some of his experiences may be those of nightmares based on the subjective impressions of anger, hate and resentment. In this life man is expressing moods, feelings and ideas which he takes to sleep with him every night. Upon awakening he fulfills the impressions of his subjective mind. He has forgotten many of the moods or feelings that he took into the deep of himself a month ago or a week ago, and he now looks upon any injury as an accidental occurrence. He calls incidents which occur matters of chance or coincidence.

This, of course, is not so. All is Law. "Nothing is lost in my Holy Mountain." Our objective experiences on this plane are the manifestations of subjective impressions. The law is the same on all planes. When we leave the objective plane, we have subjective experiences based on all subjective impressions carried over by us. This is a dream state, just as real as the plane you left.

5

Subjective Mind Impressions

When we speak of mind, we usually refer to two phases of the one mind, objective and subjective. In broad general terms the difference between man's two minds may be stated in the following terms. The objective mind reasons, analyzes, dissects, divides and chooses. It takes cognizance of the objective world through the media of the five, physical senses. It is the outgrowth of man's physical necessities. Furthermore, it may be said to be his guide where his material environment is concerned. Its highest function is that of reasoning. *It is not creative.* "I can of mine own self do nothing." (JOHN 5:30). It is "the Father that dwelleth in me, he doeth the works." (JOHN 14:10).

The subjective mind of man is that which creates and gives form to all impressions made upon it through suggestion or feeling. This phase of man's mind takes cognizance of its environment by means independent of the physical senses. It perceives by intuition. It is the storehouse of memory and the seat of the emotions. It is the Father that doeth the works. It performs its highest functions when the objective senses are in abeyance, as in meditation. It sees without the use of the natural organs of vision. It can leave the body and assume another body and travel to distant lands.

In the absolute sense, man's subjective mind does not have to travel anywhere as the whole world is within it. "Be still and know that I am God." (Ps. 46:10). God does not travel—He is Omnipresent. The subjective mind has the power to read the thoughts of others in the minutest detail. It can read the contents of sealed letters and of books locked in a safe. All wisdom and knowledge are locked within it, because it is the Higher Self of man or God.

For purposes of clarification we will say that the real distinction between the two minds consists in the fact that the "objective mind" is merely the function of the physical brain. On the other hand, the "subjective mind" is a distinct entity, possessing independent powers and functions. It has a mental organization of its own, and is capable of sustaining an existence independent of the body. In other words, it is the Soul. The most important point to remember is that the subjective mind accepts every suggestion given to it, no matter how good, bad or absurd without the slightest hesitation or doubt.

Man must, therefore, learn to entertain only good suggestions, ideas and moods. This is imperative due to the fact that man's subjective mind is amenable to the control of his objective mind, as well as to the suggestions of others. Through discipline he learns to reject all suggestions at variance with that which he wants to hear. The subjective mind expresses the feelings impressed upon it. This is the Law of cause and effect. The cause is the mood, and the effect is the manifestation of the mood.

In the subjective dream state we meet loved ones and we visit places thousands of miles away. This is real, because man is a psychological being and not bounded by space or time. Other people may tell us important things in our dreams. Tigers, lions and other wild animals talk in foreign languages to us, and it seems natural and logical while we are dreaming. However, it is when we awaken to this world of "make-believe," that we think our dream experiences are illogical or unreal. Life on this plane is truly a dream and nothing but a dream.

Is it not foolish to say man is suffering? Can God suffer; can God grow; can God expand; can God contract? It is the illusion of growth, the illusion of travel, the illusion of time and the illusion of suffering or death. If you have a toothache, who is suffering, you or the tooth? If you are hypnotized, for example, and the suggestion is given that "there is no pain," immediately the pain leaves you. On awakening you have no sense of pain. Where did it go? It was only an idea, belief or opinion accepted by your consciousness. A counter-suggestion removed it.

People talk about thousands being killed. Can God die? Can man die? God cannot be slain; neither can man be slain. God as man will come again. When we awaken—and we are beginning now to remove the scales from our eyes—we will truly become one with God, and shed His light, Love and Beauty to all the world.

We can only conjecture as to the length of time the process of awakening will take. On the other hand if time is not, it must only be the illusion of time. It may appear to be a year or a day, or eight hundred years—for in consciousness a thousand years are as a day. God is the eternal now. He is the God of the living and not of the dead.

Let us reason together. If the world is within you, where can you go? The world you will experience for a time in the after-life will be that of your crystallized beliefs. It will be a dream-world peopled by your prejudices, ideas, opinions and beliefs about peoples and things. Our ideas and beliefs are like individuals—they live and exist as long as we sustain them in our consciousness.

"Why seek ye the living among the dead?" There are no dead. All your loved ones, closest friends, all men, women and children who make their exit from this plane are very much alive and functioning fourth dimensionally. They cannot be seen by the three dimensional mind of man.

This recalling of the lost preserves the beauty of thought without limitation. In other words we must never grieve or mourn for loved ones. On the contrary we must give, "...Beauty for ashes, the oil of joy for mourning, the garment of praise for the spirit of heaviness." (ISAIAH 61:3).

By dwelling on the qualities of love, kindness, inner beauty and nobility of thought that was theirs, we resurrect these qualities within ourselves. This is what is meant by praying for the dead. It is a "holy and wholesome thought to pray for the dead." Recognizing the Oneness or Wholeness, we realize that the loved one who has passed on is still alive and dear to us. Meditating occasionally on the fact that the departed are dwelling in a state of peace, beauty and love, we change any nightmares they may be experiencing (due to subjective impressions carried over with them) to lovely experiences.

We make them whole or "holy" by our prayer which is scientific prayer. This is what is meant by giving the oil of joy for mourning. Instead of feeling that they are dead and gone—that their grave is where the body is—let us, by our inner mood, see them dwelling in a state of indescribable beauty; then we truly give the dead "Beauty for Ashes." Under no circumstances must we ever dwell in the mood or feeling of lack, limitation or regret.

6

Hearing and Seeing

Every day of our lives we are only meeting our beliefs. Let us not be fooled, cajoled or tricked by any seemingly miraculous stories or strange phenomena. Many so called strange occurrences, projections and voices are nothing but subjective manifestations. The ghosts we fear are those that walk the gloomy galleries of our mind.

To the intuitive or sensitive person the subconscious is an open book. He reveals the contents of your subconscious to your conscious or waking self. The thoughts and feelings of man can also be read by a deck of cards, sand or other devices. From time immemorial man has given certain values to cards and other symbols. Since man has given authority and power to these things, they must confirm his beliefs symbolically. By getting into a partly subjective or passive state, it is possible to reveal the contents of the subjective mind of a person. The cards, or the marks on the sand serve as an alphabet which, when pieced together intuitively, give a language that will be understood.

We are surprised many times that what is delineated is true, and many of the predictions do occur. To read the character of any individual, it must be done intuitively or in a partially subjective state. If a person is highly intuitive, he tunes in with you and reveals the contents of your subjective mind. Your conscious mind becomes aware of what you formerly were not aware.

As long as man worships at the shrine of graven images and molten idols, so long will he be a slave to his beliefs. Like the surge of the sea, he will be tossed to and fro—"a double-minded man, unstable in all his ways."

What Isaiah or the prophet of God says is only too true, "Thou art wearied in the multitude of thy counsels." (ISAIAH 47:13). He is looking for a God outside of himself; he is worshiping constantly at the shrine of the false gods. Whatever man accepts as true becomes a subjective reality. The subconscious mind of man, being absolutely impersonal, no respecter of persons and non-selective, accepts whatever man believes to be true and gives it form. The latter becomes an embodiment, an experience or condition in that man's world.

He is impressed by a suggestion that he will have an accident on the 15th of next month, and that he should avoid auto travel or train travel. This man lives in fear until the 15th; then he decides to lock himself in a room. Having impressed his subconscious with the belief in an accident, and having actuated it by fear, he knows it now must come to pass. He cannot escape. Something happens—he slips in the bathroom and hurts himself or he cuts his hand with a knife—perhaps a fire breaks out; something *must* happen.

Now, if man knows the Law of life and the Truth of Being—that "I and the Father are one" and that "whatsoever ye shall ask in prayer, believing, ye shall receive" (MATTHEW 21:22)—this man will shape and mold his own destiny. He will laugh at all dire predictions because he knows his consciousness to be God. What he feels as true of himself must come to pass. Not liking what he has heard, he says to himself, "How would I feel were the opposite true?" Then he enters into the spirit of it—gets into the mood that all things are possible to him who believes—enters into the conviction that it is so, and thrills to it. This man has actualized a new state subjectively, and this must come to pass.

If a man believes that he must get hay fever this year, as he always has in the past, let him dispel all such beliefs in powers apart from himself. Let him turn his attention to the God within—yes, turn inward, towards the Real. *This is the internalization of consciousness.* In this state let him dwell in the feeling of perfect health—enter into the spirit or mood of being healed—and he will express health.

God is truly the known God. As Paul says, "If haply they might feel after him and find him . . ." Yes, all that man has to do is enter into the feeling of the answered prayer. His eyes, ears and all his faculties must be turned inward and focused on the One, the Beautiful and the Good. While man is still in this meditative and relaxed mood, he will write on his consciousness the words of Scripture, "It is finished!" We must walk the earth knowing and believing perfect health is ours.

There is absolutely no one who can predict with accuracy for the spiritual man, or the man who "dies daily" through scientific prayer. It cannot be done because this man predicts for himself. The mystic sees the fallacy of fear of the unknown and belief in evil. The mystic, the truth student, who believes in God as taught in the Bible and prays scientifically to the God within himself, is the true prophet. Truly he prophesies for himself all the good that is to come. He is the master of his fate and the captain of his soul. He knows that God shall wipe away all tears and that there shall be no more crying.

When man awakens to the truth, he realizes that Christ is his consciousness. Then he recognizes the great Oneness wherein all men are One. Moreover he knows and understands the meaning of the greatest commandment, "Hear, O Israel; The Lord our

God is one Lord." (MARK 12:29). What such a man feels as true of himself, he feels as true of the other. He only sees and feels the good for every living creature.

Such a man is a type of Christ and is capable of seeing or hearing only good for all men. He knows that negative feelings towards another disturb the harmony of the whole or oneness of which he is a part. The whole of God is in the part, for consciousness cannot be divided. "And all mine are thine, and thine are mine; and I am glorified in them." (JOHN 17:10). "And for their sakes I sanctify myself, that they also might be sanctified through the Truth." (JOHN 17:19).

The true prophet or mystic enters into the mood or feeling of the answered prayer. He has the feeling that it is done, and closing his eyes and ears to the world, he comes before His presence with singing. He enters into His gates with thanksgiving and into His courts with praise. Contemplating the reality of the wish fulfilled, he rests. This is the Sabbath or rest of the Lord or Law. By sanctifying himself he makes others whole.

The mystic walks the earth unmoved, unchallenged and unshaken in his conviction that his feeling, "thy will be done," must be manifested. In a little while, perhaps he is still speaking, it appears—the divine image becomes visible on the world's screen. For the first time he becomes consciously aware of it. He has looked "within" and not "without" and found the wisdom, the power and the glory.

Man does not believe that it is possible for him to extend his faculties of sight so that he may actually see, for example, one of his loved ones thousands of miles away, and carry on a conversation as if they had met on the street. Neither does the average so-called wise man of the world believe it possible to carry on a conversation at a distance of thousands of miles without the aid of all the well-known mechanical inventions for this purpose.

In the chapter on "Time and Space" is outlined the remarkable ability of an Indian boy to stop the flow of blood. This same boy, in addition, had the amazing capacity of projecting his voice thousands of miles to Colorado. He did this quietly, and at the same time replies came back through the air in the voice of his brother. It was just as if two persons sat in their living room and conversed.

This is how he did it. He would sit down, close his eyes and begin to talk to his brother named Two Moons. The conversation concerned family ties, health of the mother, death of some friends and some local news. All of his comrades thought he was faking. Some accused him of being a ventriloquist and said they could prove it. They decided to have him ask three questions rapidly which would require a fairly lengthy reply. They stuffed his mouth with a handkerchief, and sealed his lips with adhesive tape. The answers came clearly over the air. These answers were heard by many men present, including the author.

After a lapse of a few minutes his brother in Colorado said, "Why don't you reply?" In answering he had asked him a question regarding a dog named "Sanco." No answer could be given as it was physically impossible for him to open his mouth. To sum it up, this Indian boy believed that he could talk and be heard at a distance only by his brother and father. This was a childhood conditioning based upon belief.

If he could project his voice thousands of miles over mountains, through fog, winds and waves, certainly he should also be able to project his vision and actually see his brother. He could not do that since he had not been informed when he was a boy that he could. His father believed that he, the first born in their family, could talk over distances to male members of the family only, and that their replies would be heard; yet his brother did not have the power, according to him, of initiating a conversation.

This may all seem peculiar and somewhat weird, but it shows in a striking manner what belief can do. If we would believe now that we could walk on the waters, we could do so. Most of us would *like* to believe or want to believe. However we do not really believe we could, simply because our mother and our teacher said, "That is impossible." Now it is a fixed belief in our subjective mind.

The storms at sea, the tempests, cyclones and hurricanes are within man himself. When we are truly at peace others will say, "What manner of man is this, that even the winds and the seas obey him?" (MATTHEW 8:27).

7

Prayer and Force

Many ask this question, "What shall I do after praying?" "What physical footsteps are necessary?" If you listen to the Voice within, and subjectively hear the answer, which is the feeling, "that it is done," "that it is finished"; then you have literally heard the answer to your prayer. A prayer is a wish to which you have acceded.

When you have fixed the things you want in consciousness (it may be health, peace of mind, love, wisdom or material things), the subjective mind of you will compel you to take all the necessary footsteps to the fulfillment of your dream or wish. You will actually be compelled to do all that is necessary to the fruition of your ideal. You will not ask Tom, Mary or anyone else, as to what you shall do or what you shall wear. No, you will do everything automatically, led by the SELF within. You can call it "being intuitively led," "divinely guided" or whatever term you wish to use. It is a compelling force which, if listened to, is the "divinity that shapes our ends."

After meditation or prayer, if you are still in a quandary, and feel like asking others for advice as to what you should do or where you should go, it means you have not believed. You have not fixed the reality of your desire or prayer in your consciousness. You will know what to do, where to go and what questions to ask. Whatever you do will be exactly according to the "Pattern on the Mount."

When man ascends into the Mount (a high state of consciousness), and enters into the joy that would be his if his ideal or dream were now realized, he has created a Pattern in the Mount. The likeness and image of the pattern appears. Man being both objective and subjective, will do whatever is objectively necessary to the fulfillment of his divine goal. He may seek a teacher. If he does it will be the proper one. He may be led to a library and find the book that will give him the desired information. He may overhear a conversation that will answer his prayer.

These are the objective manifestations of subjective impressions. "I have ways ye know not of." ". . . neither are your ways my ways . . . For as the Heavens are higher than the earth, so are my ways higher than your ways." (ISAIAH 55:8–9). "His ways are past finding out!" (ROMANS 11:33). The disciplined man, the sincere truth student, does not ask how, or when, or in what manner or through what source his good will come. When the gift appears, he instinctively and intuitively recognizes it, accepts it and says, "Thank you Father." "Father, I thank Thee that thou hast heard me and I knew that thou hearest me always." (JOHN 11:41–42). Many pray to God and then ask others to predict the future for them. Had they prayed believing, they would know the future. They would have prophesied for themselves. They would have had the silent inner knowing of the Soul—the awareness that it is—the sensation of having touched "something" within.

Man may not be able to describe his feeling in words as it is a subjective mood, which is the language of the Soul, but he knows that he knows. How can you describe a fourth-dimensional feeling in a three-dimensional language? When he perceives it objectively, he uses the King's English to describe it. This is the experience of everyone who has prayed successfully, whether on the battle field, in the streets or in the privacy of his home.

"Go (tell no man,) and shew John." (MT. 11:4). John is the world. When your prayer is answered objectively, you show it to the world and your outer senses confirm the conviction that you have entertained within. Such a person does not consult anyone as to the outcome of his wish. He knows himself what the outcome is. He has prophesied and being the true prophet, not the false one, he knows that "HE never faileth."

Those who are consulting strange gods as to their destiny are looking for a sign. You are told in the twelfth chapter of Matthew, ". . . There shall no sign be given to it, but the sign of the prophet Jonas." This refers to the eternal trinity by which all things are created—consciousness, your ideal and the feeling or nail that joins it. The mystic steps to be taken in all metaphysical demonstration include consciousness desiring, uniting with the thing desired and loving it. These steps will fulfill the Law and take you into the Holy of Holies.

8

False Prophets

The false prophets are those people who tell us there is a way out by cheating, lying and by brute force. The way out is through PRAYER; this is the way to overcome all obstacles, impediments and the challenge of the world. "All things, whatsoever ye shall ask in prayer, believing, ye shall receive." (MATT. 21:22).

Inasmuch as prayer accomplishes all things and is the answer to all problems, man's whole life should be prayer. There is nothing but prayer. We do not gain the ear of God by vain repetitions. By entering into the "secret place," which is our consciousness, and communing with our Father Who sees in secret, He will reward us openly. We must touch, through feeling, the reality of the desire for which we pray.

On hearing Truth for the first time, many maintain their old beliefs and still wish to accept the new. As a result, there ensues a quarrel in consciousness and they become neither hot nor cold. This double-minded man, who is unstable in all his ways, cannot hope to receive anything from God.

Man must leave the old with all its works and pomp. He must forget all the idols and false prophets and become the true prophet.

The false prophet believes his future depends on circumstances, conditions, environment, influences and forces outside himself over which he has little or no control. The man who believes in powers outside himself is calling God "Baali"—a God of caprice and vengeance, a God of wrath and an inscrutable being whose playthings we are. This type of man conjures a being dwelling in space who must be appeased by sacrifices, fastings, pilgrimages and repetitions of various prayers.

Man must begin now to call God "Ishi," which means "my husband, my lover." Yes, God must be your true lover. You must be close to Him, you must embrace Him. He is a God of love, of justice, of wisdom and power. We must look upon the God within us with love, understanding and absolute trust. We must not regard Him with a sense of fear, doubt and apprehension. He is not the unknown God. "In Him we live, and move, and have our being" (ACTS 17:28). Let us look upon Him as the known God.

A question often asked is, "Why is it that predictions regarding future events in my life have come to pass?" Follow the answer to the question carefully and it will be easily understood, and not appear mysterious and strange.

"I am the Alpha and Omega, the beginning and the ending, saith the Lord, which is, and which was and which is to come, the Almighty." It is possible for an intuitive person who is in a psychic, passive or receptive state, to tap the contents of the subconscious of another and reveal these "secrets" to the conscious mind or waking self of man. In other words, in a passive state, a sensitive or highly intuitive person tunes in with the fears, phobias, fixations, desirable states, subjective acceptance of marriage, divorce and various other impressions in the other—be they what they may. The individual who is tuning in with your subjective feelings translates moods and beliefs in his language and foretells accordingly.

We must remember that the subconscious mind is a storehouse of memory, and many suggestions have been accepted of which the conscious mind is wholly unaware. These are brought to the surface by an intuitive individual, and we may become aware of them for the first time. Many times, of course, these things come to pass—for whatever the subconscious has been impregnated with will be objectified in man's world sooner or later unless changed by prayer. Any man, receiving a suggestion or prediction regarding himself of an undesirable nature, can prevent this prediction from coming to pass by prayer. In this way he becomes the true prophet.

The intuitive person who made the prediction saw or felt the beginning and having seen the beginning saw the end; for the beginning and the end are the same. "I am Alpha and Omega, the beginning and the end." (REV. 21:22). There is no mystery about it, no trick and no phenomenon. All is according to the laws of mind.

It is possible to predict with a certain degree of accuracy for a person, a group, a race, a nation or the world, because the majority of human beings do not change very much. They live with the same old beliefs, same old traditions, race concepts, the same hates, phobias and fears. They follow more or less a set pattern, which can be easily read by one tuning in psychically or intuitively with the mass consciousness.

What is strange about men such as Nostradamus who tapped the consciousness of the race in the 16th Century and, from the fixed beliefs and moods of the race mind, saw the beginning and the end? Today we are witnessing the drama of the end—at least to some extent. Why should not man be able to peer through the unnumbered centuries and see all?

The prophecies of Nostradamus—or any other man—would mean nothing and could be defied and proved untrue, if men knew how to pray. Through prayer they could change their subconscious and consequently their destiny. Prayer eliminates fear, doubt and hate from the subconscious of man. That is how he weeds his garden so that only beautiful flowers may grow.

The spiritual man refuses to hear something he does not want to come to pass; he changes the beginning by a new concept of himself and, therefore, he changes the end. This is done by the law of substitution or prayer. *Instead of praying something out of existence, he prays the condition he wants into existence.* He becomes a producer.

By illustration, suppose a man is informed that someone dear to him is very ill and may die within a certain time. If he has accepted this as a fact of consciousness and sustains the belief, it must come to pass. Let us further assume the man hears of this principle and applies it, believing in the Law of Reversal. Immediately the false prophecy is nullified and the true prophecy of Life is fulfilled. The prophecy was false because it foreshadowed gloom, doom and disaster. In this way he changes the prediction and defies all the dire prophecies of man concerning things to come.

This is the process to use: first, he must change his conception of the loved one and feel and see him as a radiant being, perfect in health. This is done in a silent meditative mood by calling the subjective image of his loved one before him. He causes the person to smile, to tell him that he never felt better in his life, and that the spirit of God is permeating every atom of his being. He thrills to this annunciation and is happy because "it is so." Dwelling on the joyous answer to his prayer, he goes off to sleep in the arms of the Lord, who receives his gift and objectifies it in a little while. This man has replaced the fear of sickness and death for his loved one with the realization of perfect health. It must be fulfilled.

Whether for good or ill, the Law of the Lord is perfect. It is "a Tree of Life" to those who know how to pray. It is the "Valley of the Shadow of Death" to those who pray amiss.

Let me give you another example: A man heard the false prophecy that his child had only a few hours to live. "The thing I fear most has come upon me." The fear of death causes death. The fear of loss is "Alpha" and death is "Omega"; the beginning and the end are the same. Man changes the beginning and brings about a new end by seeing, feeling and believing his child to be perfect.

In the subjective mood of prayer he lifts the child up—actually sees him running around, playing, enjoying himself and radiating health and happiness. He actualizes this state by feeling and contemplating the psychological reality of it. He rests on this conviction. The new "Alpha" or beginning is that silent inner knowing, the conviction that all is well. It is the joy of the answered prayer. The new "Omega" or ending must be perfect health. The fear is replaced by love. "As within, so without."

By changing our mental attitude, the outer picture must change, too. "Be ye transformed by the renewing of your mind, that ye may prove what is that good, and acceptable, and perfect, will of God." (RO. 12:2). "Thou shalt love thy neighbor as thyself." (MATT. 19:19). *This is the law that will change your world.* No one can prognosticate for a spiritual man. He shapes his own ends, because "he dies daily" to the untrue. He prays unceasingly. The mystic, or spiritual man, through prayer and meditation, changes the subconscious part of his mind. Prayer wipes out fear and purges the subjective Self of all false ideas and superstitions which have been causing all the trouble. Let us face the facts and realize that every condition, circumstance, or experience in our lives is the outpicturing of a belief in the subconscious.

We must also realize that all sickness, accidents and disease of every nature are the embodiments of negative ideas or fears in our subconscious. Always remember, ". . . Though your sins be as scarlet, they shall be white as snow; though they be red like crimson, they shall be as wool." (ISA. 1:18).

9

Far-Seeing

The following is an experience of the author, which may answer many questions in the minds of the inquiring reader. He wanted to go to a certain city in the Orient in the capacity of a chemist for a large, international, chemical organization with which he was at that time associated. This is the procedure that he used: he relaxed in an armchair in the back of an old church which still stands; closed his eyes and became still. The writer imagined himself in the Orient by an inner perception of a typical Oriental setting. He felt the tropical breeze on his face and actually felt his toes being cooled off by the salt water on the sands of the seashore. He dwelled on this realization for two or three minutes, and felt the joy of being where he wanted to be. At the end of five minutes contemplation, the words of the prophet Isaiah came to his mind: "So shall my word be that goeth forth out of my mouth: it shall not return unto me void, but it shall accomplish that which I please, and it shall prosper in the thing whereto I sent it." (ISA. 5:11).

The sequel to this prayer is very interesting. A short time afterwards, the opportunity came to the author to visit the Orient. All arrangements were made to proceed by plane. However, the morning preceding his departure for the Orient, in a dream, came the vivid realization of things to come in two or three years hence. A friend appeared in the dream and said, "Read these headlines—do not go!" The headlines related to war. The writer "dreams literally."

The subjective mind of man always projects a person whom you will immediately obey, because you trust and love that person. To some people a warning may come in the form of a mother who appears in a dream. She tells them not to go here or there, and gives the reason for the warning. Your subjective is all-wise. It knows all things. It will speak to you only in a voice that your conscious mind will immediately accept as true. It would not be someone whom you distrusted or disliked. Oftentimes the voice of a mother or loved one may cause you to stop on the street, and you find if you had gone another foot, a falling object from a window might have struck you on the head. This is not the voice of your mother, or teacher or loved one. It is the voice of your subjective and it speaks in a tone or sound that you instantly obey.

As proof of this, I questioned my mystic friend. He assured me that he knew absolutely nothing about the warning "he" had given me subjectively. No, it is man's subjective that is ever portraying the drama of its contents in the form of a dream or a vision of the night. If man suggests to himself that he will remember and understand the symbolism portrayed therein, he will know the outcome of many things. He will also learn to change the dreams; for by changing his consciousness he changes the dream, and as he dreams, so shall he become.

Joseph was warned in a dream. God spoke to Solomon in a dream and offered him his choice of gifts. Solomon chose wisdom, and God added long life and riches. With all our getting, let us get understanding of this principle; then our pillars of strength will be the two great pillars—"Boas and Jachin"—Wisdom and Understanding.

Possessing the wisdom which the Bible teaches, and the understanding to apply the psychological principles therein, man's
inner righteousness will show itself in his world. He will need no
man-made rules of conduct to guide him; for he will be led by the
wise Power within him. If the thing that you now want will bless
yourself and others, it is the Divine Will. "I am come that they
might have life, and that they might have it more abundantly."
(JOHN 10:10). "Heretofore have ye asked nothing, . . . ask and ye
shall receive, that your joy might be full." (JOHN 16:24).

In prayer realize the great oneness and feel the end of the
answered prayer. The Being within you sees the beginning and
also sees the end. It shows you the end in a feeling, "In a dream,
in a vision" or by a voice. Listen to It. It will talk to you. Obey It,
because It is Wisdom speaking to you. "In a dream, in a vision
of the night, when deep sleep falleth upon men, in slumberings
upon the bed; then He openeth the ears of men, and sealeth their
instructions." (JOB 33:15–16). ". . . He giveth to his beloved in
sleep." (PS. 127:2).

The writer, in consequence of his dream, immediately canceled
the trip, cashed the tickets and sought no reason. He was under
subjective compulsion to do so. A subsequent event—the tragedy
of Pearl Harbor—proved the truth of the Inner Voice. "Trust in the
Lord with all thine heart." (PROV. 3:5). Thus shall ye walk in the
land, verily ye shall be fed. Let him be a "lamp unto my feet." (PS.
119:105).

10

Missing The Mark

Our sin is in missing the target of perfection. Though in the beginning the archer misses his target a thousand times, he gains skill through the practice of aiming again and again at his mark. So does the fruit of sin, which men call punishment, perfect the skill of His chosen one. An ancient meditation points out, "Sin and punishment are one and the fire of punishment is the fire which refineth My works." "Even in the sinner I AM the actor and I, too, am the sufferer, in the experience of punishment. Thy pain is My pain, thy suffering My suffering. Thy sorrows pierce My heart, thine anguish is My anguish. I stand not aloof, unmoved, watching my handiwork as a potter watcheth the clay upon its wheel. Nay, not so, for I am clay, and the wheel, and the potter too. I am the work and the worker, and the means of working."

"The delusion of separateness passeth with the completion of the work for which I enter into manifestation and because nothing can prevail against Me even the worst of sinners shall come in their appointed time to liberation."

Yes, all men shall see the Light. When man awakens to his true Self, he will experience the radiance of the Light Limitless, and from the field of sin and punishment he shall pass into the bound-less freedom of the divine perfection. Let us realize the Truth of the following verse from Arnold:

"*Never the spirit shall die.*
The spirit shall cease to be never.
Never the spirit was not.
End and beginning are dreams.
Birthless and deathless and changeless—
Remaineth the spirit forever.
Death hath not changed it at all.
Dead though the house of it seems."

11

Oneness with God

I am the Lord, and there is none else, there is no God beside Me."
(ISAIAH 45:5). You, the reader, are the one and only being there
is. When you say "I AM," that means the sum-total of all the per-
sonalities in the world. All other conceptions are projections in
space of the one being, yourself. In the Bible, which is a text book
on psychology—metaphysics and man's moods and feelings—the
"I AM" is constantly referred to as, "I am the way, the truth,
and the life." (JOHN 14:6). "I am the Resurrection and the Life."
(JOHN 11:25). "I am that I am." (EX. 3:14). These and similar say-
ings shine forth in all their true brilliance when once we see that
Jesus, the Christ, was not speaking of Himself personally, but of
the principle of Being inherent in all mankind.

What Truth students fail to see is that there is only one man,
for the same reason that there is only one God. God and man are
one—"I am in the Father, and the Father in me." (JOHN 14:11). You
cannot divide the One; infinity cannot be divided or multiplied.
The seeming divisions are the illusions of separation. We must give
recognition to that innermost Self which is pure Spirit, and which
is not subject to any condition whatsoever. We feel that we are con-

ditioned by time and space, but these conditions have no place in essential Being. The true recognition of the "I AM" is the acknowledgment of the Self within you. God, the Father, eternally subsisting in His own Being, sends forth all forms of His will. Likewise, all forms return to the formless One, according to an immutable law.

You, the one man, can comprehend the infinite Self within you by a limitless expansion of your conception of God. You thus return to the Universal Being as a son coming home to his father. The more we study the Bible the more we realize that, by the art of meditation—i.e., by going inward—we become greater in our knowledge and comprehension of the mysteries contained therein. The road inward is the road to greatness, the Royal Road of the Ancients, and for all men who desire to become united with the Supreme Cause, the root and substance of all.

Rebirth means to ascend inwardly from the lesser to the greater by an inner realization, or by the lifting up of consciousness from one step to another. The consciousness, being lifted up by contemplation, dwells on the fact that I am now the being I long to be, and to make it real I must feel it. This realization is an inner awareness of the new state of consciousness or rebirth.

There is not a single note that was ever played that any man cannot play. Anything that has ever been felt by any holy man, any man can feel. There are no facts or secrets hidden in the dim past that any man cannot bring to light. You are the only Being there is. You have a memory of all that has passed, consequently all tones, moods, vibrations, knowledge and wisdom are within you. There is no language that ever was spoken that you cannot speak. There is no voice that you cannot reproduce, because all is within you.

YOU have always lived! "Before Abraham was, I AM." (JOHN 8:58). "When all things cease to be I AM." You, man, wrote the Bible! You may have forgotten it, but if you meditate on its passages, the subjective self within you will reveal to your conscious mind what you meant, when YOU wrote it thousands of years ago.

Time is an illusion; God is the eternal NOW. Thousands of years are as an instant. Aeons are as a day. Therefore, shed now the belief in time and the idea that we have to come back again and again to this earth plane—one time as John, another visit as Mary—in order to gain more experience, to perfect ourselves and become as Jesus, the Christ.

We are sometimes told that it is almost impossible for us to become as Jesus, or Moses, or Elijah in one lifetime; it takes several lifetimes; moreover, many say that we have some "karma" to work out in this life. In other words, we must expiate for the sins and crimes committed in past lives before we can be purified. Some state that it is almost impossible to change certain physical conditions in this life, particularly, if one happened to be born with a congenital disease or deformity.

This teaching is false and a contradiction of everything the Bible teaches, namely, "Behold, I am the Lord, the God of all flesh: is there anything too hard for Me?" (JER. 32:27). "I will restore health unto thee, and I will heal thee of thy wounds, saith the Lord." (JER. 30:17). "... Who healeth all thy diseases; Who satisfieth thy mouth with good things, so that thy youth is renewed like the eagle's." (PS. 103:3, 5). "I will ransom them from the power of the grave, I will redeem them from death." (HOSEA 13.14).

A cripple is not instantly healed because of his or your belief. Likewise, if a man's leg is amputated, the reason he does not grow another leg is because his father and mother, the authorities of certain text books, plus tradition and race belief, all contributed to the false belief and teaching he received as a baby. He holds a firm conviction within himself now that God cannot grow another leg for him. He firmly believes that nothing can be done for him except to wear an artificial leg. "Thy faith hath made thee whole." (LUKE 8:48).

Regarding the belief of some people that we must suffer for errors of the past or for sins committed centuries ago, there is no basis for this false concept. If a person believes that he must suffer for something he has done, he will suffer. It is all based on belief.

The only loss, limitation, restriction or evil in the world is our belief in loss, our belief in limitation, our belief in restriction and our belief in evil or disease. This is known as "the son of perdition" or sense of loss spoken of in the Bible. "Come now, let us reason together, saith the Lord: though your sins be as scarlet, they shall be white as snow; though they be red like crimson, they shall be as wool." (ISAIAH 1:18). "And their sins and iniquities will I remember no more." (HEBREWS 10:17). "For thou, Lord, art good, and ready to forgive; and plenteous in mercy unto all them that call upon thee." (PS. 86:5).

The reader should stop, think and realize for a moment that a God who says, "Love your enemies, do good to them that hate you," by necessity of His greater Love, blots out all of the past. He wipes away all tears, and forgives you immediately. Can you imagine a God asking you to forgive those who trespass against you, and in another breath refusing to forgive Himself? "He shall call upon me, and I will answer him." (PS. 91:15). "I, even I, am he that blotteth out all transgressions for mine own sake, and will not remember thy sins." (ISAIAH 43:25).

Man completely detaches himself from the past by partaking of a great psychological and mystical feast of peace and happiness. Realizing the presence of God within him, he rises in consciousness to the joyous conviction that he is NOW the being he longs to be. Having fixed this state within him, a silent inner knowing possesses him; all former doubts and fears pass away and shall be remembered no more. By sustaining this silent inner feeling, that which he felt inwardly becomes expressed outwardly.

12

Forgiveness

Your consciousness is God and there is no other God. If a seeming wrong or injury has been committed against you, therefore, you must forgive. Now, there is no other—so there is no other to forgive. You give something for the feeling of resentment or hate that you now hold in your consciousness. You give way to a feeling of love, peace, harmony and joy.

In other words, it is the age old law of substitution in consciousness. To "forgive" means to give something for. If you have a headache, and you take a pill for the condition you are giving yourself something for the headache. Likewise a person who happens to be in a mood of resentment must replace this mood he is entertaining by forgiveness. The only way he can forgive himself for entertaining such a negative mood is by the indwelling gift of love and peace within his own consciousness.

You must radiate this feeling to all around you. When you think of John or Mary, who formerly was what you thought the "cause" of resentment, you will see the Christ in him or her and rejoice. You become exceedingly glad that they are expressing all they long to be. You are seeing the Truth behind the form, the

Divinity behind the mask. "Love thy neighbor as thyself," says Jesus. Your neighbor is yourself. All love is to oneself. All treatment is to oneself, consequently all hate, jealousy and bitterness is to oneself. If you decide to hate someone, or injure someone, whom are you injuring? Yourself only! "I am The Lord that is my name: and my glory will I not give to another. (ISAIAH 42:8). As is well known, many people are healed by absent treatment, and the teacher or healer does not know anything about the details of the case in question. The blending of the patient with the healer is not essential. The Scriptures point this matter out clearly. Jesus raised Lazarus who was dead four days. A dead man cannot ask you to pray for him or blend with him; neither can the insane ask you to heal them; yet the Scriptures reveal that they were healed.

The only reason the disciples could not heal an insane child was because of their unbelief. If you wish to treat a person at a distance, even though he has not requested you to do it, you must feel the reality of the healing within yourself. You actualize this state within your subjective mind. Since there is only one subjective mind, what you have felt as true of the others, must be manifested in the other's world. There is no other, for there is only the One.

This question comes up occasionally wherein someone says, "Oh, I had a remarkable spiritual healing, but some weeks or months later there was a relapse to the former state." No teacher or healer can guarantee the continuance of the healed state, due to the simple fact that man is not an automaton, but has freedom to choose. He has freedom to be sick or well as he chooses. The day following the healing, he may re-infect himself by accepting a suggestion of fear or by entering into an emotional outburst of anger or hate.

Man must change his habits of thought and adopt for his rule and guide: *right thinking, right feeling and right action*. Teaching is healing; consequently a very important function of the healer or teacher is to point out to the sick person the cause of his trouble and how to eliminate it. The sick person, realizing that all his troubles of whatsoever nature were effects of causes set up within himself, must decide to discontinue the wrong thinking which produced the ill effects in his world. He learns that the Christ within can accomplish all things. Having learned the causes for the misfortunes and chaos in his world, he will then maintain the consciousness of health, peace and harmony. He will, thereby, prevent a relapse or re-infection of former destructive moods.

In the eleventh chapter of St. Mark, we read these wonderful words: "What things soever ye desire, when ye pray, believe that ye receive them, and ye shall have them". (MARK 11:24). There are no conditions laid down. It is not necessary that one be a holy man or a great mystic to manifest the innermost desires of his heart.

The man we call the murderer, thief, or the person of ill repute could, if he desired, become Jesus, the Christ, instantly. Shocking as this may sound, all that such a being would have to do—according to the law of spiritual consciousness—is to forget completely the past by turning within; feeling with all his heart and soul that he is the Christ and is doing the works of Christ Jesus on earth. As a man thinketh in his heart, so shall it be done to him. In the twinkling of an eye he could be changed.

Paul, according to the New Testament, persecuted his fellowmen, testified against them, and had them put to death. He is a shining example of the state of consciousness that can be attained instantly if desired. Paul was illuminated on the road to Damascus by turning within, changing his conception of himself, and finding that he really was the Christ. We can do this! If this is not true, the whole teaching of the Bible collapses and is false. *But it is true,*—"the same yesterday, today and forever."

The truth is we are all that we ever will be now, but we fail to recognize it. The mass murderer or the violent assassin can in one moment become the Christos, the illumined one. This person need merely rise in consciousness to the conviction or feeling that he is the Christ, and doing the works of Him that sent him.

We are told the story of the boy born in the stable, of lowly parents. We are informed that He was a carpenter. It was said, "Can there any good thing come out of Nazareth?" (JOHN 1:46). Yet this boy, born with all the social and worldly handicaps, became one with the Father. He walked the earth the God man, seeing only perfection, beauty, order, symmetry and proportion in everybody and everything. Why? *Because by uplifting his consciousness these qualities were established and made manifest within himself.* "What thou seest, that thou beest." The meaning of the story of Jesus is that any man, woman, boy or girl can become the Christ. The command is, "Go thou and do likewise." The Jesus Christ state of consciousness is not born of woman, but comes *out* of the imagination of man. We must refuse to believe the idle, foolish statement that it takes man one hundred or one thousand years to become a Jesus. There is no time in God. "That which is to be hath already been." In other words, you are all that you will ever be NOW—yes, this very instant. Even fifty million years hence will not make any difference to the Reality within you.

Do you not realize the everlasting Truth of the ages that you are God, individualized in a fleshy body? All conceptions that you ever conceived or will conceive, all growth, learning, wisdom, expansion and contraction are the illusion of growth and expansion. God cannot learn or become wise. He is All-wise. He knows all. Hence it must be the illusion of evolution. It is simply the grand masquerade of the One.

Yes, there are deep, heavy scales on our eyes. If we will let the scales fall, we will see the light within. Our prayer should be, "God give me eyes to see the Light." "Awake thou that sleepest, and arise from the dead, and Christ shall give thee light." (EPH. 5:14). If you think for one moment that you are unworthy to see the Light and become the perfect man, then dwell on these words: "But if the wicked will turn from all his sins that he has committed, and keep all my statutes, and do that which is lawful and right, he shall surely live, he shall not die, all his transgressions that he hath committed, they shall not be mentioned unto him: in his righteousness that he hath done he shall live." (EZEKIEL 18:21, 22).

13

Outpicturing Man

All outer manifestations of man's life are projections of an inner state or image contained within his consciousness. Man must learn that the only way to create a better world is to build the constructive images within his consciousness that he wishes to see expressed in the world. The world is an outpicturing of our mental beliefs and attitudes.

We look at a man and we say that he is lame, deaf, blind, ragged or poor. We have clothed him in rags, in garments of blindness, deafness and poverty, but in absolute Truth he is God and can never be any less than He is. Let us awaken from the dream, and clothe every man in the garment of Christ, the Anointed One. "Who is blind as he that is perfect and blind as the Lord's servant?" (ISAIAH 42:19).

The perfect man cannot see a blind man or a deaf man; neither can he see any man in rags. He sees only divine perfection, the divine idea behind all form. He sees the everflowing reality, justice and beauty in all things. In other words, he sees God in all things. He does not see another. His command is that of a King: "Take ye away the stone." (JOHN 11:39).

The perfect man, giving complete, recognition to God and realizing that all things are possible to Him, cannot see any lack anywhere. Hence his request for abundance is automatically granted. He is blind to all evidence of the five senses and worldly beliefs or powers outside of himself. His eyes are forever turned inward towards the Real.

If you have a lesion on your face, and a friend prays for you, the latter does not inwardly see the lesion on your face. On the contrary he hears you telling him that you are overjoyed that God has granted you a perfectly beautiful, smooth face. If he succeeds and the scar disappears, "he saw the perfect face." This manifestation may have occurred the same moment you were telling him the foolish details of the difficulty you experienced so far in treating it, and all the resultant failure. Where did the lesion go? Where did it disappear to? The truth is that it existed only in your imagination and belief.

When you have learned these great truths, you have "reincarnated" indeed. To learn these truths is to know them, and to know them is to live them and witness them. Man is playing a role in the great drama of life. When the curtain comes down, he puts off his garment, hangs it up and disappears from sight. He ultimately returns to the Source. From Him we all come forth—to Him we all at last return. There is no other place to go. "They shall not hurt nor destroy in all my holy mountain." (ISAIAH 11:9).

When John or Mary "dies"—as we usually employ the term—it means that John or Mary, as the case may be, lives on in each one of us. A person never dies. The quality, tone, or mood of the Infinite, which was his always existed and always will. The subjective afterlife may be a nightmare or a lovely dream—depending entirely on what man has impressed on his subjective mind before passing over. Let us play the melody of God here, and listen to the overtones of life. In this way we will be better equipped to play the game of life in the next dimension.

All things subsist in the Infinite and when we call forth the expressions by our feelings, then it may be said to exist. "I am Alpha and Omega, the beginning and the ending, saith the Lord, which is, and which was, and which is to come, the Almighty." (REV. 1:8). "... I girded thee, though thou hast not known Me." (ISAIAH 45:5). We fail to see that it is always God coming into the world when a child is born. That child is its own father and mother. There is only the One Father and He is "Our Father." "It is He that hath made us." (PS. 100:3).

14

Inequality of Man

It does not make any difference whether man was born deaf, dumb or blind, the "works of God" can now be made manifest. The Divine Love of God in action is omnipotent in healing. It is invincible; therefore, Jesus or the illumined consciousness can enter into the realization, "It is done." Many ask this question: "Why is an innocent child born blind, deaf or crippled?" Obviously, they have not read the Scriptures, for the same question is asked in the ninth Chapter of John: "Master, who did sin, this man, or his parents, that he was born blind?" Jesus answered, "Neither hath this man sinned, nor his parents: but that the works of God should be made manifest in him." (JOHN 9:2–3).

The work of God is the nature of God, which is goodness, truth and beauty. Man's conscious mind is "father" and his subconscious "the mother." Man creates by his feelings or moods. In the creative act, the mood at the moment of conception determines the nature of the child. "I form the Light, and create darkness, I make peace and create evil: I, the Lord do all these things." (ISAIAH 45:7). This means the Lord (law) can be used two ways, but through our ignorance we misuse it. Our moods create! What is the nature of our mood? What tone do we strike during the creative act? If there is someone in the parent's world whom they hate the sight of, or if there is a voice that they wish they would not hear again, a corresponding expression must be brought forth. A blind or deaf child will be born—as within so without—as above so below—as in Heaven (consciousness) so on Earth.

The law is impersonal and no respecter of persons. It gives to all men that which they ask according to their mood or belief. The nature is the feeling or conviction within man. If man feels he is healthy, realizing his state of consciousness as the determining factor, he cannot express illness. The child be it deaf, dumb or blind is judged good and very good, because it is the perfect image and likeness of the consciousness which produced it. ". . . Every creature of God is good." (I TIM. 4:4). "His work is perfect." (DEUT. 32:4). "And God saw everything that He had made, and, behold, it was very good." (GEN. 1:31).

You will see that whatever "tone" is struck by the parents, a corresponding voice or mood comes forth by the law of reciprocal relationship. No child is subject to so-called laws of heredity. "What mean ye, that ye use this proverb concerning the land of Israel, saying: "The fathers have eaten sour grapes, and the children's teeth are set on edge? As I live, saith the Lord God, ye shall not have occasion any more to use this proverb in Israel." (EZE. 18:2–3).

Yes, the father may be insane, tubercular or criminal, but the only thing passed on to children is the spirit or mood of the father and mother. It is possible for a so-called criminal to have a son who becomes a Beethoven, a Shakespeare, a Lincoln or a Jesus. It depends on the moods of the parents or the states of consciousness at conception. "I, if I be lifted up from the earth, will draw all men unto Me." (JOHN 12:32). If you are lifted up in consciousness to the point of acceptance or belief that your son will be the noble, dignified, Christ-like being you dream of, according to the law of reciprocal relationship a corresponding mood or quality of the Infinite comes forth.

If man realized that God walked and talked in him, he would change the whole course of his life. God is indivisible. There are not two Infinites, but only One. It is impossible to divide infinity. The whole of God, therefore, is in the seeming part of man. All beings in the world live and have their existence only in the consciousness of man.

Let us get away from any idea of separateness. Some wish an eternal continuance of themselves as John, Mary or Joe, coming back again and again for more experience. They do not realize they have experienced everything—have seen all things and have always lived.

"... The works were finished from the Foundation of the world." (HEB. 4:3). It is not the personality known as John, Mary or Joe coming back. It is always the spirit of the one God. "Elias is come already." (MATT. 17:12).

The personality, John or Mary, is simply the mask of God—it is the sum of the appetites, moods, feeling and beliefs of each of us. In other words, we tincture or color the one Spirit by our beliefs and impressions. God does not repeat himself; therefore, objectively, we look different. Subjectively we are all one. The subjective is the Real—the objective—the mask. John, for example, might have lived in New Orleans. We will say he died; then the quality which was John lives on in all beings throughout the world.

Now, during the creative act, in some part of the globe the tone or quality that was John is struck.

This could be in China or Japan or elsewhere and that quality or mood of the One God comes forth. It is not the personality we knew as John; it is ever the spirit of God. The same instant that John died, instantaneously, the same vibration could come forth in a member of another race and country.

Cycles of 500, 800 or 1,000 years have nothing to do with this law. God is timeless; all tones are in the one. When we are playing on the grand piano, it will respond according to the notes we strike. Man is the one who measures, and "the measure he metes shall be measured unto him." "Whatsoever he sows, that shall he also reap." You sow the seed in consciousness and you reap the fruit of the seed; it will be the exact likeness of the seed sown. *Let us sow beautiful thoughts; let our hands play divine melodies; let our eyes see the beauties of God; let our voices be those of praise and thanksgiving. Then surely we will reap what we sow.*

15

Time and Space

A question frequently propounded is this: "Why do I say I have been here before; I have seen this place before?" Is there any place in which you have not been? The world is within you.

You do not have to travel to any point in order to describe any place, country or area in the minutest detail. God is omnipresent; He does not travel. You are both God and man. You are both unconditioned and conditioned—the unconditioned or formless awareness is God Almighty. This is the Real Self of you.

You have forgotten who you are, and you believe that you must travel to India in order to see it. You can sit still and see all of India. "Be still, and know that I am God." (PS. 46:10). Your "I AM-NESS" is God. God is everywhere and in all things. There is nothing outside yourself. You are the center of all creation and all revolves around you. As long as we believe in travel, time and disease, we must experience them. In other words, we must have proof of our convictions.

Consider this explanation: John wishes to take a trip to Killarney. He dreams about the trip and plans for it. He buys a ticket;

arranges for passage and passport. He knows that he is going to take the trip. John goes to his Father every night and takes all his moods, feelings and beliefs with him as gifts. The Father always acknowledges whatever his son etches on consciousness.

While asleep, John's subjective has taken the psychological trip to Killarney, visited his friends and heard their voices and comments. John awakens and takes the trip physically. Eventually he motors to Killarney from Cove and does not need to ask directions from anyone. WHY? He was there before; he visited it a few weeks ago, psychologically, while asleep on his couch. Now he knows the way. He hears a voice and stops suddenly, saying loudly and excitedly, "I've heard that voice before, even that same expression." "Why I know this cottage, I've lived here before!" A dozen different expressions pour forth from him. Consciously, he has forgotten, but the subconscious is the storehouse of all memories and experiences—the seat of all knowledge.

His experience has nothing to do with previous incarnations. John has been visualizing a wonderful trip, impressed his subconscious and "went to sleep on it." His subjective, knowing all, accepted the suggestion and dwelt there psychologically. When the conscious mind arrived there, it experienced all the subjective states. "I go to prepare a place for you, and if I go, I will come again and take you unto Myself, that where I Am there ye may be also."

When he hears the voice and feels the loving caress of a dear one, it is the objectification of his own desire and then it registers. "I come to make the blind see and those that see blind." This means that all things exist now but we refuse to believe it and accept it.

For example, the writer some years ago met a boy who was considered ignorant and stupid by his comrades. This boy could not read or write, neither did he know the classics. Yet he could stop the flow of arterial blood, which flows freely, by closing his eyes and saying, "Stop it." When he opened his eyes, the bleeding had ceased. He believed that his prayer would always be answered and even though others mocked, he never failed. "Charity (love) never faileth." (COR. 1: 13–8).

That is why belief is not necessary on the part of the sick person. Yes, truly the woman can have an issue of blood for twelve years, and by touching the hem of His garment, she shall be made whole. To touch the hem of His garment means to feel the thrill of accomplishment on the inside of the subjective self.

It is the inner silent knowing. It is the feeling within that "It is done." We must always seek the end. Having felt the end, we have already determined the means to that end.

How did the so-called ignorant boy mentioned in a previous chapter have this ability? His explanation was as follows: As long ago as he could remember, his father told him that the power to staunch blood was a tradition in the family, and was handed down from father to son. The first born in the family had the gift, but the other members, such as sisters and other members, such as sisters and other brothers did not possess this power.

The boy grew up in this belief and fully accepted the fact that he could stop the flow of blood. If he saw it, he closed his eyes to it, and issued the command which was always obeyed. He really did not know how or why it should stop. He knew practically nothing about God. The reason the blood stopped flowing was because of his *belief.* (He stated that at home in Colorado he frequently was called upon to stop cases of hemorrhage.)

A very peculiar thing about this healing capacity was that he believed that he had to be present and see the blood flow, and so he could not heal anyone out of sight. Not aware of the laws of mind or the working of the conscious and subconscious faculties of man, this shows what could be accomplished with a youth if conditioned properly by someone who knows and understands the laws of life and the Truth of Being. For example, no amount of words or explanation would convince this Indian boy of the fact that he could stop the flow of blood at the request of a third person—even though he did not see the patient. This was a belief implanted in his subjective mind at an early age and he accepted it as a part of the tradition of his tribe or family.

Children, particularly under seven, are living mostly in the subjective state and very amenable to suggestion, especially from parents whom they trust and love. This boy was unconscious of the "fact" that it could not be done, just as many of us believe that the technique of stopping the bloodflow is only possible through the use of blood coagulants and a tourniquet. It is all a question of how "free consciousness" has been bound and conditioned by belief, opinion and custom.

16

The Journey Beyond

Frequently is the author asked: "Will we meet our former parents, brothers and sisters in the after-life?" In the 22nd chapter of Matthew, the question reads like this: "Therefore in the resurrection whose wife shall she be of the seven? for they all had her?" (MATT. 22:28). Jesus answered them, "In the resurrection they neither marry, nor are given in marriage, but are as the angels of God in Heaven." (MATT. 22:30).

We must not think that our former wives or husbands will be lined up to greet us. Family relationship is for this three dimensional plane. Believing in the old concept of reincarnation, just imagine what it would mean! Maybe two million wives would be waiting for us. Where there is a deep, unselfish love of a mutual nature, there will be a meeting and a joyous reunion.

When you learn to love, and are prepared to serve others, your solo will cease, as Dunne says in "New Immortality," and become part of a duet. Thus you join through love other players and produce orchestral effects. Finally one day we will discover we are playing in the symphony of all creation. There is no lost Soul and even the child that dies in the womb, still lives. Yes, it grows; expands and through love it goes from "glory to glory."

When we awaken, all are one in consciousness. In the absolute state, all tones are one. There is nothing but a great Oneness. "There is neither Jew nor Greek, there is neither bond nor free, there is neither male nor female." In God the sinner and the holy man are one. Black, white, yellow and brown races are all one. He ". . . hath made of one blood all nations of men for to dwell on the face of the earth." (ACTS 17:26).

"I am the resurrection, and the life." (JOHN 11:25). Your I AMNESS is the only living Reality. "In Him we live and move and have our being." (ACTS 17:28). An angel is an attitude of mind, a voice, a tonal quality or mood. God, being infinite, consists of an infinite number of angels or "angles." Man is God in infinite expression. There is no end to his expansion of consciousness, because God is without beginning or end.

All our friends, relations and all those people who are past and gone, are within ourselves. They are angels of heaven—and where is heaven? Jesus says, "The Kingdom of Heaven is within you." There is, therefore, no place for them to go except within our consciousness, which is God, the Absolute. "Do not I fill heaven and earth? saith the Lord." (JER. 23:24).

"There is but one God, the Father, of whom are all things, and we in Him." (I COR. 8:6). Our Father is in heaven and heaven is within us. All your loved ones, when they finally awaken, subsist in the eternal stream of consciousness as angels of God, in perfect peace, and they are one with their Father. All men, women and children in the world are notes in a vast musical composition. Let us become lost in the unity of the whole, and all sense of separateness leaves us. The sum total of all creatures does not comprise unity,—no more so than the fractions contained within the number, one, bring about the fundamental unity of that number, by being added together. We may regard multiplicity as a way of experiencing that unity. When we enter the world of Reality by a process of withdrawal into the enduring self ("I die daily"), we no longer persist as individuals, surrounded by a world which is not ourselves. *We are all that is*, and our individuality has merged in the *all*. We are the life of all creation.

The eternal continuance of John or Mary Smith as a personality is the nemesis of the uninformed. This is the point where foolishness and wisdom hopelessly divide. As long as John desires to be separate, he desires to be separate from that Universal One, who is the root and substance of all things. The universe of the foolish man is one containing spheres, planets and planes through which he passes forever—a universe becoming greater all the time.

The Truth student looks at things somewhat differently. He knows that this Spirit within him, which he is trying to individualize, is not an individual at all. He knows that the life within him has never been separate from God and never can be. What the illumined one calls "being alive" is eternal Life living in him. Man is playing against fate when he wishes to be John Smith forever. He might be referred to as an egoist, who thinks that as personal self, he is sufficiently important to subsist for aeons of time.

Let us be real Truth students. Let us realize that that which lives and abides in us, is eternal Life. If it were true that the personal John Smith was the Thinker—if it were true that he was the Life—it would be different. These are appearances due to the illusion of the material state.

In contemplation and in deep meditation, we realize these profound truths about man. It is Thought thinking him. He is not thinking thoughts. Is it not LIFE living in him? He is not living LIFE. Is it not eternity concealed or hidden within non-eternal natures? All of us are an inevitable part of the unity of God and inevitably destined to be reabsorbed into His unity. We need not fight on forever. We can "stand still, and see the salvation of the Lord." (Ex. 14:13). The absorption of the particular by the universal is the end of individual existence, as we know it on this plane of consciousness. We could liken it, as the return of the spark to the flame, the return of the water to the sea.

Man is forever asking, "What shall I be in the afterlife? What will Mary be? What will all individuals be?" We are victims of centuries of false beliefs. Over thousands of years we have begun to believe in a strange complex of separation or apartness from our Father. Yes, man is always asking, "Will we lose this individuality of ours." The word "individual" means that which is indivisible. The answer must be, "What is individuality?" Is it not the One Life looking out through the countless windows and eyes? This Life is ever at one with Itself and It shall not be anything less. Man is not an individual; he never was. His emotions, beliefs and intellect tried to make him something apart. All things in this relative world of ours are expressions of the absolute. The one life is expressed in countless modes. It is all One Reality. The one in the many, and the many in the one. The apparent separate manifestations are notes in a grand symphony. There is a difference in the notes, and they are grouped differently into chords and harmonies; yet, we must remember the symphony is One. Grace notes, somber notes and notes used to form part of a magnificent opening chord are not separate; they all are the symphony and the symphony is one and indivisible. The composition is one Reality. Every note shares the joy and beauty of every other note, and shares the Life of every other note. The life of the whole is in each note. The part is in the whole, and the whole is in the part. You are the Grand Symphony. You are the Creator and the Hymn of Creation. We are the Supreme Reality sharing the life of all things.

"Everywhere in heaven is Paradise. Even though the grace of the Chief Good does not reign there after one only fashion!" Does not this mean that the mystery of the ultimate Reality is multiplicity in Unity?

The reason for all the chaos and misery in the world today is given to us in Chapter 2 of Jeremiah: "For my people have committed two evils; they have forsaken me the fountain of living waters, and hewed them out cisterns, broken cisterns, that can hold no water." (JER. 2:13). Millions of men today pray to a God in space whom they look toward as some being living in the skies, consequently, their prayers are not answered, because they do not know how to pray. They have forsaken the God within, and have created a God outside of themselves. They also have given power and authority to conditions and circumstances.

Instead they must realize that rather than permit the world to control, influence and frighten them, they should control what now controls them. We have the choice to control our outer manifestations or be controlled. The world with all its pomp and ceremony is the cistern that holds no water and if man drinks of this, he will thirst again. He must go back to the fountain of living water and drink of it in order to become free of the limitations of matter and circumstance. Man must leave the world of sound; go back to the "Silence," and dwell in His peace, strength, wisdom and power.

17

Finding Oneself

Let us once and for all awaken from the dream of being separate. Actually, we never have been separate and never have been individuals. When we completely die to all of our false beliefs, we are back again in the Garden of Eden. "Thou hast been in Eden the Garden of God; every precious stone was thy covering." (EZEKIEL 28:13). This is the illusion removed and the Fact made known. The ancients called it the awakening from a dream. It is an awakening from the recurrent dream of self to find the "Selfless One."

". . . Awake thou that sleepest, and arise from the dead, and Christ shall give thee light." (EPH. 5:14). This means that when you awaken, you learn all has been a dream—all wars, crimes, one's mistakes and misfortunes. All the chaos of the world is a nightmare—unreal, to be forgotten and remembered no more. The reality of this awakening is to find oneself in a kingdom of love, peace and happiness with the Light of Truth always shining. Beholding the Truth, dwelling upon it, accepting and rejoicing in it, we realize that the streams of "manyness" all lead to the Oneness.

The Gospel of Good Tidings is the realization that the One alone lives, and that the One alone is the end all men are seeking, the one Self that stands supreme midst the illusions of the not-selves. Then man knows for the first time what the ancients meant in their meditations, when they said: "Neither is there anywhere injustice, and the semblance of it is the delusions of separateness. The strife, the quarrels, the contentions that thou witnesseth day by day are the plays of light and darkness which I am. All sense of effort, all semblance of exertion—know these as illusions and with thy mind's eye see Me entering into all."

One man, a friend of the writer, who has read twenty or thirty books on reincarnation, is no longer worried about which wife he will meet in after life. He said, "You know I must have had millions of wives, also fathers and mothers." He is now at peace, having read the 22nd Chapter of Matthew. He is no longer worrying about which one to claim. He was under the impression that there might be strife in heaven over him.

Man is told what the true reincarnation or rebirth means in Chapter 3 of John, "Except a man be born again (of water and the spirit), he cannot see the Kingdom of God." (JOHN 3:3). Millions have read this chapter, however like Nicodemus, they fail to see the light or true meaning. They say, "How can these things be?" (JOHN 3:9).

Obviously pouring water on the head of a person does not bring about a spiritual awakening or change of consciousness. There must be another meaning. The simplicity of Truth is its greatest stumbling block. Children who believe in Santa Claus operate this law very successfully, because they believe in "make-believe." That, after all, is what the whole world is and all things contained therein—a vast "make-believe—nothing more and nothing less.

At one time a little Spanish girl lived a few doors away from the author. He knew the family well, and often visited at the home of the little girl's parents. She was about eight years of age and attended the local parochial school. For months she had been asking her parents for a bicycle to ride in Central Park. The mother's constant answer was: "Stop bothering me. You know there is a war on and no bicycles are available." She continued to ask, however, much to the annoyance of her parents.

This little girl was a typical tom-boy, fought with the boys in the neighborhood and "got a black eye" occasionally. One night the writer of this book said to the little girl: "Mary, you can get a bicycle, and I know where." Immediately her eyes expanded and she was all ears and exclaimed, "Where?" The following dialogue took place between us:

TEACHER: "Go to bed immediately and close your eyes. Now imagine clearly that your boy and girl playmates are riding your bicycle in Central Park, and just see their smiles."

MARY: "I won't give my bicycle to anyone if I get it."

TEACHER: "Then, Mary, I am afraid you can't get the bicycle. The person who is willing to give you the bicycle wants you to share it with your playmates who have no bicycle, so that you can make them happy. He insists that you make your friends joyful and merry."

MARY: "Oh, all right, if that's the kind of person he is. I suppose I must agree."

TEACHER: "Fine, Mary, that is the proper feeling. Now, Mary, Christmas is coming shortly and there is a big boss over all the Santa Clauses, who tells them what they can give to little girls and boys who are good."

MARY: "Mother said Santa Claus could not or would not bring a bicycle."

TEACHER: "Now, Mary, your mother is very busy; you annoy her too much and she does not always realize what she says. This is the way you can get the bicycle before nightfall tomorrow."

MARY: "Really, promise?"

TEACHER: "Mary, you know I always keep my promises. I take you to the movies when I promised, and buy you ice cream when I promise."

MARY: "I believe you. Tell me how."

TEACHER: "Mary, close your eyes and imagine yourself riding a bicycle in Central Park."

MARY: "I can see the bicycle I want!"

TEACHER: "See your playmates riding the same bicycle, one at a time. See them smiling and laughing and full of fun. Now the Big Santa Clause is listening to you and is pleased, because you believe he has the power to give it to you. He is glad, also, because you are going to share it. He will give it to you tomorrow, before nightfall. Go off to sleep, sound asleep, deep, deep sleep."

About six o'clock the next evening Mary was at Woolworth's—78th Street and Broadway, New York City—when she suddenly began to cry. A lady nearby noticed this and speaking gently said to her, "Little girl, what is the matter? Did someone hurt you?" Mary replied, "No, but there was a man at our house last night and he told me the boss over Santa Claus would give me a bicycle before nightfall. It's getting dark now and there is no bicycle." The lady was moved and said: "That man had no right to promise such a thing." She took the little girl to her apartment nearby, and gave her a bicycle, which her daughter, who had died two years previously, had used. She told Mary that she always wanted to give it to a child who loved God.

This is all that prayer is—simply "make-believe." That is all "reincarnation" is. If you do not like what you are, make-believe you are that which you long to be. Accept it, sustain the mood or belief and you will embody that state. The water spoken of in the Third Chapter of John is "consciousness," and the spirit is the spirit of joy in possessing that which you long to be or to do. The Kingdom of Heaven is the peace and stillness that follows the answer to your prayer.

We are here to experience the joy of living and for no other purpose. Out of the great silence comes God, appearing as man. Man has dreamed a dream away from reality and found that which he calls evil and sin—to be an illusion of the senses. Man must return to the Silence, and in the presence of Truth all these so-called evils fade away, since they never really existed.

18

Renewal of the Mind

You may transform your mind, body and affairs through the water and the spirit (3rd John) by re-educating the subconscious (water). One way of getting at the subconscious is by affirmation; that is, saying a thing over and over again. This is the way with some; but all these affirmations are only abstractions. What is needed is something concrete—an inner perception, a firm conviction within yourself. You must actually feel yourself as the Doer and the Seer. This is the "Spirit."

If your desire is to be a great teacher of the Law, the following suggestions could be used. Close your eyes, which shuts out the evidence of your senses; still the mind by dwelling on God; ask yourself, "What does God mean to me?" The answer automatically comes—God is Love, Beauty, Infinite Intelligence, Omniscience, Omnipotence, Omnipresence and All Wisdom. Then feel yourself to be the great teacher. You must feel the reality of it; the joy and thrill must course through your veins with the mood of actual accomplishment.

It is as if you went to the theatre, came home, sat down on the couch, closed your eyes and began to review all the scenes in a contemplative mood. You hear the voices, and you see the beautiful scenery, lights and costumes. You are witnessing that which has already taken place. Prayer is contemplating the reality of the wish fulfilled and reacting to the joy that, "It is finished." (JOHN 19:30). "Enter into his gates with thanksgiving, and into his courts with praise: be thankful unto him—and bless his name." (PS. 100:4). NOW YOU ARE BORN OF WATER AND THE SPIRIT.

When we pray, it is essential that we realize nothing is achieved by desperate effort. We grow, not by trying to grow, but rather by permitting the fact of growth to assert itself or be manifest in ourselves. Man cannot become the Great Teacher or Healer by any direct effort. "The father that dwelleth in me, he doeth the works." (JOHN 14:10). The result is due to an attitude or mood of the mind that the Wisdom, which is ever present, is made manifest in us. We do not create wisdom, virtue and knowledge. We reform and reverberate these attributes by a renewal of the mind, thereby releasing ever-existing principles and qualities into manifestation.

19

Meditation

The discipline of looking inwardly is Meditation. What we understand we do naturally. What we do not understand we force ourselves to do. Students so often tell the teacher how hard they tried. The very effort meant failure, for meditation is always effortless. Tension, exertion or force result in failure.

An excellent way to still the mind is as follows: imagine yourself on a mountain top, looking into a lake. In the placid surface you see the sky, the stars, the moon and those things above the earth. If the surface of the lake is disturbed, the things seen are blurred and indistinct; thus it is with you. You are not "still"—not at peace—and the answer to prayer comes only to the man who dwells with all tranquility on the joy of already having received that for which he prayed.

Meditation is the internalizing of consciousness. It is the pilgrimage within. If an eight year old child can operate the Law successfully, we can. We first must become as the little child. Half an hour a day spent in meditation upon your ideals, goals and ambitions will make you a different person. In a few month's time the gentle, silent acknowledgment comes that God is within

you, that the spirit of Almighty God is now moving in your behalf
and that which you long to be, to possess or do is already a fact
of consciousness. Man actualizes this state by feeling the thrill
of accomplishment; when he has succeeded, he will no longer be
worried, anxious or apprehensive.

Moreover, he will not ask anyone for advice, because he will
be under compulsion to do that which is right. His subjective
mind compels him to take all the necessary steps to the completion of his goal or objective. After prayer, if a man is still doubtful
and begins to argue with himself as to which course to pursue,
it means that he has not fixed the desired state in consciousness;
then let him go back again and dwell in the reality of it.

"Verily I say unto you, Among them that are born of woman
there hath not risen a greater than John the Baptist: notwith-
standing he that is least in the kingdom of heaven is greater than
he." (MATT. 11:11). This means that any man who prays successfully and touches Reality by getting into the proper mood or
feeling is greater than the wisest man. Most of us live life looking outwardly. The wise learn to look inwardly. The disciplines of
looking "inwardly" are termed together, "Meditation."

Detachment is the key to meditation. That is, we must sever
ourselves completely from all worldly beliefs and opinions, and
focus silently upon our ideal state. It is the effortless-effort which
causes us to flow towards that which we realize without conflict.
Detachment does not mean that we give up what few earthly possessions we may have. It means that we must give up possessiveness in ourselves, or release the attachments that peculiarly limit
us to a human viewpoint in all matters.

"Be still and KNOW." Stillness is not only keeping quiet; it
means that the causes within the Self, by which the inward life is
rendered discordant, have been removed. It indicates that there
must be no inner dissonance, but rather when man goes within
himself, he must find perfect and abiding peace. Knowing that God

is within himself makes man live in a world that is ever peaceful. The lack of it makes him live in a series of conditions which grieve him to the end. He fusses about things which, if he saw them differently, would not cause one moment of unhappiness.

Every day of our life we should meditate on beauty, love and peace. We should feel that these qualities are being resurrected in us. As we meditate daily on this inner beauty, let us feel that we are Jesus the Christ, the illumined man. Let us actually conjure the mood that would be ours were we actually doing his works and healing the blind, the halt and the lame. As we walk the earth, we must sustain this mood or conviction that we are Jesus and those qualities, which he portrayed, will be resurrected within us. They were always within us! This state of consciousness is not born of woman. *Jesus is born out of the imagination of man and nowhere else.* It is the second birth or spiritual awakening of man.

The birth of Jesus the Christ truly takes place in man as he practices the disciplines and meditates on the ideal state.

By moving inward, the mystic finally finds the Real. As he goes inward he realizes first that this thing called the body is very unreal, and this earth upon which we are seated becomes unreal. The external life becomes the dream; the internal life awakens and moves further and further inward. Finally it seems to merge, and suddenly the meditating Self perceives that, by going inward, it has found the Universe. The suns, moon, stars and planets are within. For the first time he knows that planets are thoughts; that suns and moons are thoughts; and also he apprehends that his own consciousness is the realization which sustains them all. Temporarily in space are moving the dreams of the Dreamer; worlds, suns, moons and stars are the thoughts of the Thinker. His eyes are closed; He is meditating, and we are His meditation. It is CONSCIOUSNESS meditating on the mysteries of Itself!

This inward journey ultimately leads man to the Real. It leads man away from the sense of the small "I" to the realization of the eternal Self. The mystic's mind, through meditation, finds the peace, the strength and fortitude for further steps. The practice of the discipline of meditation bestows beauty, love, peace, grace and dignity upon every impulse, every attitude and every act.

In conclusion, let us meditate on these lines, written by the finger of God, the Ancient of Days, which have come to us, down through the ages—ever the Ageless Wisdom:

"Of all existence I am the source, the continuation and the end. I am the germ, I am the growth, I am the decay. All things and creatures I send forth. I suppose them while they yet stand without, and when the dream of separation ends, I cause their return unto myself. I am the Life, the "Wheel of the Law, and the Way that leadeth to the Beyond. THERE IS NONE ELSE."

Quiet Moments With God

Contents

Condensed Interpretation
of 23rd Psalm

❧·❧

The Lord is my shepherd. I sing the song of the jubilant soul for I have chosen God as my shepherd. Divine Intelligence rules and guides me in all my ways. I shall not want for peace, harmony, or guidance because God's Wisdom governs me. I lie down in green pastures always, since God is prospering me beyond my wildest dreams. I find myself beside the still waters as I claim the Infinite Peace of God floods my mind and heart. My emotions (waters) are stilled and calm. My mind is now serene and it reflects God's Heavenly Truths and Light (my soul is restored.) I think of God's Holy Presence within me all day long. I walk the path of righteousness through my devotion and attention to God's Eternal Verities. I know there is no death and I fear no evil. I know "God has not given us the spirit of fear, but of love and power, and a sound mind." God's rod (Love) and staff (Truth) comfort, sustain, and nourish me. The banquet table of God is always set before me; it is the Secret Place of the Most High, where in my thought I walk and talk with God. I eat the nourishing Truths of God whenever fear and worry (my enemies) trouble me. The bread I eat is God's idea of peace, love, and faith in all things good. The meat I eat is the Omnipotence of God; the wine I drink is the essence of joy. The Wisdom of God anoints my intellect; It is a Lamp unto my feet and a Light on my path. My cup (heart) is truly the chamber of God's Holy Presence; it runneth over with love and joy. I mentally dwell on Goodness, Truth, and Beauty; this is my House of God.

Condensed Interpretation of The 91st Psalm

—❧·❧—

I dwell in the Secret Place as I contemplate God and His Glory within me. I abide in the Shadow always because I know God's Love surrounds and enfolds me making straight, beautiful, and joyous my way. The Lord (The Spiritual Power) is Sovereign and Supreme, the Only Power. It responds to my thought; It is, therefore, my Refuge and my Fortress. This Spiritual Power inspires, heals, strengthens, and restores my mind and body. It is God. It is a Beneficent, Kindly Power. I trust It completely, and It responds as mercy, love, inspiration, and beauty. This Divine Power covers me with Its feathers of Love, Light, and Peace. It is wonderful!

I completely reject the negative thoughts of the world (the arrow by day), and God's Love dissolves the fear-patterns of my subconscious (terror by night). I know I am secure in the Invisible Hands of God. I always vibrate with the Mind of God and all is well. I am completely free from fear of accidents or hostile activities (pestilences that walketh in darkness) because I know I am immunized and God-intoxicated. I have received the Divine Anti-body—the Presence of God in my heart. The thousands of negative thoughts and suggestions of the world are destroyed consciously and subconsciously, for God walks and talks in me, and I live in the joyous expectancy of the best. (There shall no evil befall thee). God and His Holy Angels (God's Ideas, Impulses, Intuition, and Guidance) have complete charge over me, and I am safeguarded in all my ways—in health, right activity, self expression, and Divine companionship. By contemplating the Presence of God, I tread upon the lion and adder (obstacles and complexes of all kinds). My salvation (solution) is revealed to me as I think of God and Heaven; then all the Divine force hasten to minister to my eternal joy.

Healing Treatment

The gifts of God are mine. We are gathered together in the Presence of God from whom all blessings flow. I use every moment of this day to glorify God. God's Harmony, Peace, and Abundance are mine. Divine Love flowing from me blesses all who come into my atmosphere. God's Love is felt by all present here and His Love is healing them now.

I fear no evil for God is with me. I am always surrounded by the Sacred Circle of God's Love and Power. I claim, feel, know, and believe definitely and positively that the spell of God's Love and Eternal Watchfulness guides, heals, and takes care of all members of my family and loved ones.

I forgive everyone and I sincerely radiate God's Love, Peace, and Good will to all men everywhere. At the center of my being is Peace; this is the Peace of God. In this Stillness I feel His Strength, Guidance, and the Love of His Holy Presence. I am Divinely guided in all my ways. I am a clear channel for God's Love, Light, Truth, and Beauty. I feel His River of Peace flowing through me. I know that all my problems are dissolved in the Mind of God. God's ways are my ways. The words I have spoken accomplish that whereunto they are sent. I rejoice and give thanks realizing my prayers are answered. It is so.

How to Forgive

❧·❧

Forgiveness must take place within your heart and mind to be the real thing. *To forgive* means "to give for." Give yourself the feeling of love and good will instead of the mood of anger, resentment, or hatred. Your mental attitude governs your experience. Keep your mind clear, poised, serene, calm, and full of an expectancy of the best. If you resent another, you are giving too much power to that other and hurting yourself. *To forgive* is to change your thought, and keep it changed. Use the following technique in forgiving another: Whole-heartedly, sincerely, and lovingly pray for the other mentioning his name. Pray: "God is prospering him. The Peace of God fills his soul; he is inspired and blessed in all ways." You rejoice that the Law of God is working for him, through him, and all around him. Do this until your heart and mind are so full of love, there is no room for resentment. You are now free.

Group Healing Prayer

❧·❧

We are gathered together in the Presence of God. There is but One God, One Life, One Law, One Mind, and One Father—Our Father. We are all brothers and sisters as we have a common Father.

I salute the Divinity in each person here this morning. The Love of God flows through me to all those present here and to all people everywhere. I believe and know that the Omnipresent Power and Intelligence of the Infinite One moves through every individual here, and that he is positively, definitely, physically, and mentally healed. I know Divine Right Action is taking place in every cell, organ, tissue, and function of each person manifesting as peace, harmony, and health.

I believe that Divine Guidance is being now experienced by every one in this congregation. God—the Great Counselor—leads each of us to ways of pleasantness and paths of peace.

The words which I speak now shall accomplish what I please and prosper whereunto they are sent. I rejoice now and enter into the mood of thankfulness knowing my prayer of faith is fulfilled.

Be Still and Know

❦

Be still and know that I am God. I now still the wheels of my mind as I think of God and His Love. My emotions are controlled perfectly; I am serenely calm. My mind is at peace and it reflects God's Heavenly Truths and Light. The Wisdom of God rises to my surface mind as I am still and calm, revealing to me the perfect plan, showing me the way I should go.

My devotion and attention are focused on God's Eternal Verities all day long. I constantly claim that God's Wisdom, Truth, and Beauty rule and guide me in all phases of my life.

God's rod (Love) and staff (Truth) sustain, nourish, and strengthen me in all endeavors. Whenever fear comes, I immediately turn to God and His Holy Presence rejoicing in this Truth: "God hath not given me the spirit of fear, but of Love, and Power, and a sound mind." I eat of the bread of heaven, made of peace, harmony, and faith in God. My prayer is, "Lord, evermore give us this bread."

Drive In Peace

This is God's car. It is God's idea, and it moves from point to point freely, joyously, and lovingly. God's Wisdom guides this car in all its ways. God's Order, Symmetry, and Beauty govern the mechanism of this car at all times. God's Holy Presence blesses this car and all its occupants. The driver of this car is an ambassador of God; he is full of love and good will to all. God's Peace, Truth, and Understanding always govern the driver. God directs all decisions, making straight, beautiful, and perfect the way. The Spirit of the Lord-God is upon the driver, making all roads a highway for his God.

Seaman's Version of the 23rd Psalm

The Lord is my Pilot; I shall not drift. He lighteth me across the dark waters; He steereth me in the deep channels; He keepeth my log. He guideth me by the star of holiness for His name's sake. Yea, though I sail 'mid the thunders and tempests of life, I shall dread no danger; for Thou art with me. Thy love and thy care they shelter me. Thou preparest a harbor before me in the homeland of eternity; Thou anointest the waves with oil; my ship rideth calmly. Surely, sunlight and starlight shall favor me on the voyage I take, and I will rest in the port of my God forever."[*]

---

[*] (By J. Rogers, a merchant marine captain, written during World War II.) Published by Navy Chaplains Bulletin, Washington, D. C.

King's High Way

◆·◆

W e will go by the king's highway, we will not turn to the right
hand nor to the left."

My way is God's way, and all His ways are pleasantness and all
his paths are peace. I travel under God's Guidance led by the Holy
Spirit. My highway is the Royal Road of the Ancients, the middle
path of Buddha, the strait and narrow gate of Jesus. My highway is
the King's Highway, for I am a King over all my thoughts, feelings,
and emotions.

I send my messengers called God's Love, Peace, Light, and
Beauty before me to make straight, beautiful, joyous, and happy
my way. I always travel the King's Highway meeting God's messengers of peace and joy wherever I go. I go by the mountain-top
road, knowing that with mine eyes stayed on God, there is no evil
on my pathway.

Whilst driving a car, riding on a train, bus, airplane, or on
foot, God's Spell is always around me. It is the Invisible Armor of
God, and I go from point to point freely, joyously, and lovingly.
The Spirit of the Lord, my God, is upon me, making all roads a
Highway for my God. It is wonderful!

Prayer for Driving and Traveling

◆·◆

A nd the Lord, He it is that doth go before thee." My Domi-
nant mood of faith and confidence is that God's Wisdom and
Power always rule, guide, and govern me in all ways. This feeling is
the Lord that goes before me. My conviction of God's Presence is

strong and mighty, and I know the Spiritual atmosphere in which I dwell goes before me, making straight, beautiful, joyous, and happy my way. I know that whenever I travel by bus, train, airplane, automobile, or whatever means of conveyance I use, God's Love and Intelligence guide and govern my journey. All the highways and byways of my world are controlled by God, making the skies above and the earth beneath a highway for my God.

Perfect Eyesight

My eyes are God's eyes, and I see perfectly. The Living Intelligence which made my eyes is now controlling the processes and function of my eyes and my entire body. I know and believe that my vision is Spiritual, eternal, and indestructible. "If, therefore thine eye be single, thy whole body shall be full of Light." This means I see only the Truth; I love the Truth; I know the Truth. I see God in all men and in all things. I see Spiritually, mentally, and physically. My eyes reflect the Glory, Beauty, and the Perfection of God. It is God looking out through my eyes seeing His own ideas of Perfection. My eyes are the windows of my soul; they are pure and are kept single to Love, Truth, and Beauty at all times. The Harmonizing, Healing, Vitalizing, Energizing Power of the Holy Spirit permeates every atom, cell, nerve, tissue, and muscle of my eyes making them whole, pure, and perfect. The Divine, perfect pattern is now made manifest in my eyes, and every atom and cell conform to God's perfect pattern on the Mount. Thank you Father.

His Holy Presence

❖

I am God, and there is no God beside me. I am checked by neither time nor space. I am held by no bonds of name or form. I am present everywhere. I am thy God and Lord of countless hosts. I am in the Holy of Holies, in the Heart of the True Temple on the Holy Mountain. I commune with God now. His Love and Light flow through me, and I am flooded by the Radiance of the Light Limitless. I am lifted up and inspired; I am expanding into the Divine Bosom of the Father. I smell the Sweet Fragrance of God; this Inner Perfume touches my heart strings; it beats to the Melody of God. I place my faith in the Divine Presence and Perfection of He Who Is. My Higher Self is God; He communicates to me; I hear the Inner Voice. It illumines, inspires, and elevates me; periodically, I find myself in ecstasy, immersed in His Holy Omnipresence. Now I know I am a son of the Living God. I am Divine Spirit—a child of God; in Him I live, move, and have my being. I know He is meditating and I am His meditation.

Love's Healing Balm

❖

By this shall all men know that ye are my disciples, if ye love one another." God is the Absolute Lover; hence it follows that before the appeal is made, the answer is given. The Love of God flows through me now; I am surrounded by the Peace of God; all is well. Divine Love surrounds, enfolds, and encompasses me. This Infinite Love is inscribed in my heart and written in my inward parts. I radiate love in thought, words, and deeds. Love unifies and harmonizes all the powers, attributes, and qualities of God within me. Love means joy, peace, freedom, bliss, and praise. Love is freedom. It opens prison doors and sets free all the captives. I am radiating love towards all, for everyone represents the Love of God. I salute the Divinity in the other. I know and believe that Divine Love heals me now. Love is a guiding principle in me; it brings into my experience perfect, harmonious relationships. God is Love. "He that dwelleth in love, dwelleth in God, and God in him."

The Power of God

God is the only Presence and the only Power, and I am one with It. God's Strength is my strength; His Intelligence floods my mind. This new awareness gives me complete dominion in every department of my life. I am now joined to the One Universal Mind. His Wisdom, Power, and Glory flow through me. I know that the Energy and Power of God permeate every atom, tissue, muscle, and bone of my being, making me perfect now. God is Life and this Life is my life. My faith is renewed; my vitality is restored. God walks and talks in me. He is my God; I am one with Him. The Truth is my shield and buckler; I rejoice that it is so. Under His Wings shall I trust. I dwell in the Secret Place of the Most High and I abide under the Shadow of the Almighty.

The Peace of God

—✖—

And into whatsoever house ye enter, first say, Peace be to this house." My mind is flooded with the Life, Love, and Truth of God. Whenever my attention wanders away from God, I bring it back to the contemplation of His Holy Presence. I enter into the Secret Chamber within me—my own consciousness. I am in Heaven; I am perfectly quiet, calm, serene, and poised. "Peace be within thy walls, and prosperity within thy palaces. For my brethren and companion's sakes, I will say, Peace be within thee." I live in the House of the Lord, my God, and I seek only the good. I am living in His Kingdom. I feel and sense the Divine atmosphere of peace, love, and joy. I stir up the gift of God within me. I know that I and my Father are one; I sense and feel the reality of this; His Life flows through me. I know that in His Heaven, where I live, move, and have my being, all my prayers are answered. I am at peace. The Dove of Love has whispered in my ear, "Peace be still!"

My Inner Peace

—✖—

My mind is still and at peace; I reflect the Wisdom and Beauty from on High. The Spirit of God flows through me now in thought, word, and deed; I am at peace. The peace that passeth understanding fills me. I sense and feel the security and tranquillity of my mind, which is in tune with the Infinite. I rest in the Everlasting Arms. My life is God's Life, and It is perfect. I am one with my Father, and my Father is God. Poise, balance, and equilibrium are mine now. My mind is God's mind, and it is perfect. God's ideas constantly unfold within me, bringing about harmony, health, and peace. I know the Spirit of Truth is leading me into all Truth. I am poised in the knowledge that God is, and all there is, is God. I radiate the sunshine of God's Love. Love is the fulfilling of the law, and the law is I am that which I contemplate.

Letting Go

I now relax and let go. I am at peace. The peace that passeth understanding fills my mind. There is peace in my home, my heart, and in all my affairs. I let go completely because I know there is a Power responding to me as I speak. This Power flows through me; it vitalizes every atom of my being. I radiate good will to all mankind. My thoughts are God's thoughts, and God's Power is in my thoughts of good. "Be still, and know that I am God." I am still and quiet now because I realize and know that the only Presence and the only Power indwells me. It flows in my behalf; I am at peace, and all is well. Peace, be still. I see the Truth; I love the Truth; I know the Truth. I know that in peace and in confidence lies my strength. His Life, Love, and Truth flow through me now, and I give thanks that "It is done."

Poise and Balance

My mind is full of peace, poise, balance, and equilibrium. There is a deep, inner serenity within me. I am calm now;

I am filled with a sense of peace and Divine justice. There is a Divine solution to all my problems; I give thanks. I dwell in the Secret Place of the Most High and I abide under the Shadow of the Almighty. He is my Refuge and my Salvation. "My God; in Him will I trust." I rejoice in receiving the ideas of God; I am at peace. I know that Infinite Intelligence leads and guides me in all ways. "The sons of God shouted for joy." I am a son of the Living God, and all that the Father hath is mine. I know the Truth; I love the Truth, and I rejoice in the Truth. The Spirit of Truth leads me now into all Truth. I am always thinking rightly. I reflect Divine Wisdom and Divine Intelligence. "With mine eyes stayed on thee, there is no evil on my pathway." My eyes are on the good, and all good is mine. I hear the voice of God; I am at peace.

A Spiritual Treatment

All is Spirit and the manifestation of Spirit. My life is God's Life; I am perfect now. All my organs are God's ideas, which minister and benefit me. I am a spiritual being: I am a perfect reflection of the Perfect God. I feel and know that I am perfect in all ways; I am Spiritual, Divine, and Holy. I am one with my Father, and my Father is God. I am expressing harmony, peace, and joy. All growth in my body and affairs is governed by Infinite Intelligence which is the Active, All-Wise, Law-Abiding Principle called God. I know that I am immersed in the Holy Omnipresence, and every atom, tissue, muscle, and bone of my being are flooded with the Radiance of the Light Limitless. My body is God's body; I am whole and perfect. I am one with God. My mind is flooded with the peace that passeth understanding, and all is well. I thank thee, Father.

Speaking the Truth

I realize and know that when I speak, it is God speaking through me. God speaks by means of man. My words are "apples of gold in pictures of silver." "My words are spirit and they are life. My words are spirit and they are truth." I know the Truth, and the Truth sets me free. My words are full of life, love, and feeling. When I speak, I give joy and happiness to all. I am a messenger of God; I bring glad tidings to all; I speak in peace. God's ideas constantly unfold within me, and they bring harmony, joy, and peace to me. I express myself powerfully and confidently. I am the perfect articulation and expression of Truth. I speak the Truth, love the Truth, and know the Truth. Infinite Intelligence speaks through me now. I now decree a thing, and it shall come to pass. Thank you, Father.

Spiritual Medicine

A merry heart doeth good like a medicine, but a broken Spirit drieth the bones." I am ever joyous, active, and energetic. I am always passing on God's ideas to my fellow man and I give him peace, joy, and happiness. "In thy presence is fullness of joy; at thy right hand there are pleasures for evermore." "The joy of the Lord, is my strength." I am always cheerful, free, and full of happiness. I have dominion over all things in my world; I sense and feel my oneness with God, with life, the universe, and all things. I am perfectly adjusted emotionally. I meditate on whatsoever things are lovely, good, wonderful, and Godlike. The Peace of God is mine now, and I stir up the gift of God which is joy. I am a son of the living God, and "all the sons of God shouted for joy!"

My Faith Makes Me Whole

—❧·❧—

I am spiritual. I am faithful to God or Good. I love only the Good. I am the consciousness of God and reflect His wholeness, completeness, and perfection. I reflect the Perfection of God in every atom of my being. My heart is merry; it maketh a cheerful countenance. My body is God's body; it is perfect now. I am expressing harmony, health, and peace in all the departments of my life. The Light of God shines through my eyes; I see the Truth perfectly. My life is God's life; it is perfect now. It flows through me joyously, harmoniously, and peacefully. The Love of God wells up within me; I express perfect health. I am full of joy and happiness; I am full of confidence and faith. My faith is my inner feeling and conviction that I am whole and perfect. God is the Eternal Now; my good is right this moment. My faith hath made me whole.

Faith In God

—❧·❧—

Jesus said, "Thy faith hath made thee whole." My faith is my inner feeling and conviction that God is, and all there is, is God. I have a joyous expectancy of the best; I know only good can come to me. "Faith is the substance of things hoped for, the evidence of things not seen." Even though I do not see what I want, I know that all things come forth from the Self-Originating Spirit within me. I now turn to God; I think of His qualities, attributes, and aspects. I realize that all these qualities are within me. As I contemplate His Presence, I know peace, order, joy, love, perfection, purity, and holiness flow through my mind and body now. I rejoice in this realization and I give thanks that it is so. I sense and feel my oneness with God, with life, with the universe, and with all men. My faith is in the Law of Good. Right is might. Yes, the right use of the Law of Good or God is mighty over all. I now call things that be not as though they were, and the unseen becomes seen.

Your Health

God walks and talks in me. He is my God and He is Perfect. The Spirit within me is ever Perfect, Whole, Happy, and Complete in Itself. I now reflect the Glory and Beauty of the Perfect God. The Light of the One Who Forever Is shines through me and all around me; every atom of my being dances to the rhythm of the Eternal God. My heart is merry; it maketh a cheerful countenance. My words are as a honeycomb; they are sweet to my soul and health to my bones. The Light of God shines out through my eyes; the Love of God wells up in my heart. I know that I do all things through Christ which strengtheneth me. My body is God's body; it is perfect now. The Divine Self within me—right this moment—gives me perfect health, happiness, and harmony. God keeps me in perfect peace. "Father, I thank thee that thou hast heard me. And I knew that thou hearest me always."

Overcome Doubt

·❊·

I know the Truth which sets me free. God is the Truth, and I am expressing God in all ways. I do not doubt my relatives or friends. Each one of them is expressing God now; I see the Christ in all of them. I give them freedom because I know all belong to God. Divine Love in me causes me to know that I shall receive nothing but Divine Love. I trust my friends, since I trust the God in them. I put away all sense of selfishness and possessiveness. I know Divine Love in me sees the Divine Love in my friends. I salute the Divinity in the other; I am at peace. I know and understand the Truth of Being. I believe only in good. There is nothing but God and His world. I am governed by God. All around me are perfect, spiritual, Divine beings. I love to work with others. I love to represent and express God's ideas; I rejoice in receiving God's ideas in exchange. I am full of joy and happiness, for I am the infinite joy of God. All my fellow-workers are my brothers and sisters. I bless them all. I know they are prospered in all ways. I am full of confidence and faith.

Cast Out Fear

·❊·

I have absolute trust in God; I expect the best; I know only good can come to me. Divine Love in me casts out all fear; I am at peace. I see the Presence of God everywhere; I am absolutely fearless; God is with me always. If God be for me, who can be against me? I know that one with God is a majority; this heals and frees me from all sense of fear. Only God's thoughts come to me; these thoughts continually unfold, bringing me harmony, joy, peace, and success. I am the consciousness of God; I am surrounded by Divine Love. I think rightly on all occasions. God's Power is with my thoughts of good. His Love. Life, and Truth flow through me; I am immersed in His Holy Omnipresence. I am always surrounded by the Infinite Peace of God. I am full of Divine Understanding. Divine Love goes before me to make straight, perfect, and joyous my way. God walks and talks in me; I know I am one with my Father; my Father is God. I have faith in God; therefore, I fear not. "Fear not, little flock; for it is your Father's good pleasure to give you the Kingdom."

Overcome Resentment

❧

I know that all men are my brothers. All of us have a common Father. I see the Living Christ in everyone I meet. I salute the Divinity in each person. The Love of God flows through me to all mankind. I bless all those who criticize me. I pray for those who speak ill of me. I rejoice to see others succeed. I loose everyone now and I let them go in peace. I open the windows of my mind; I let in the influx of the Holy Spirit. I am perfect and cleansed. I am at peace. The Love of God fills my mind; all is well. I reflect the Love of God; I am absolutely loving toward all. I am conscious of God everywhere because God is over all, through all. I know that the action of God is taking place in the mind and hearts of all. It is wonderful!

Overcome Grief

Man is spiritual and he lives forever. There is no death; all is Life. God is Life and that Life is my life now. I cannot lose that Life. I cease now to grieve over loved ones, for I know they live forever. Where God is, there is no evil; there is only God. I am not separated from loved ones because there is only one Mind and one God. In Him we live, move, and have our being. We are all expressions of the one Being—the one Consciousness. I am instantly in touch with my loved ones, for Spirit is Omnipresent. Every idea that comes to me is from God; these ideas reflect His Beauty and Truth, and they make me absolutely joyous. "The sons of God shouted for joy." I rejoice now to receive God's Truth. "In thy Presence is fullness of joy." Only God's ideas come to me and to my loved ones; all is well.

Overcome Confusion

I know that all things are made by the self-contemplation of Spirit. I am at peace. Peace is the Power at the heart of God. The Self of me is the Living Spirit Almighty. I am full of infinite potentialities. The God-Self fills my mind now with ideas of beauty, perfection, and poise. I have the key to happiness and growth. I am the temple of God; the Spirit of God dwelleth in me. I am never confused because God's ideas unfold in my mind with perfect sequence. All of God's ideas are always available to me; they minister to me and heal me. I am Divinely inspired; my only thoughts are God's thoughts which are perfect, whole, and beautiful. My mind is full of poise, balance, and equilibrium. My mind is the Mind of God. The ideas of God give me joy, happiness, peace, and harmony. "In Thy Presence there is fullness of joy."

True Friendship

I have found my Divine Companion, and He is God. He is fixed in my heart. He walks with me; He talks with me; He tells me I am His own. It is wonderful! I have found my Spiritual friends within; their names are love, joy, peace, gentleness, goodness, faith, meekness, and temperance. These are the only important friends. They are the veritable Almighty Power of God walking in my form. Having found the companions within, I now attract by an Immutable Law people who blend with me spiritually. I radiate friendship and love to the whole, wide world, and to all mankind! I love, and I am loved by everyone. I love people; I am interested in their welfare and happiness. I realize all men are my brothers, and all women are my sisters. I give the best in me to people; they in turn find enjoyment and pleasure in my presence and company. I am now attracting wonderful friends by the Universal Law of Love; God is love. I kiss God now in a mental embrace, for He is my Beloved.

My Divine Companion

—≷·≷—

I and my Father are one. I know that God is the very life of me. I feel secure now, for I know that Life, Love, and Truth are all within me. I am never alone; God is always with me; "His rod and His staff comfort me." This Inner Presence, the God-Self in me, walks and talks in me. Having found my True and Everlasting Companion within me, I can never lack for wonderful companions in the without. God is the Fullness of all things. My Divine Friend is closer than breathing; He is nearer than hands and feet. I radiate love and friendship to the whole, wide world, and the world responds in kind. I am loving; I am kind. I have a wonderful companion now. This companion blends with me spiritually, mentally, and in all ways. It is wonderful! The Love of God flows through my thoughts, words, and deeds. As within, so without. I have found my Divine Companion within and I now recognize him on the without.

Buying And Selling

—≷·≷—

I am aware that there is a perfect law of supply and demand. I practice the golden rule in all my affairs. I am at peace. Whatever I wish to sell is an idea in the Mind of God. The Principle of All Knowledge is within me. I know everything that I need instantly. I recognize whatever I wish to buy or sell represents an exchange of ideas in Divine Mind within me. I know there is mutual satisfaction, harmony, and peace. The price is right; the people are right;

all is in perfect order. I know the Truth; I understand the Truth, and I am the consciousness of God in action. All the ideas I need constantly unfold within me with perfect sequence and perfect combinations. I receive and rejoice in Divine ideas and I give them to my fellow creature; I receive ideas in exchange. Peace is mine now. There is no delay in Divine Mind; I accept my good.

Money—God's Idea

I know that money is an idea in Divine Mind. It symbolizes wealth; I recognize it as a means of exchange. All God's ideas are good. God created all things; He pronounced His creation good and very good. Money is good; I use it wisely, judiciously, and constructively. I use it to bless mankind. It is a very convenient symbol; I rejoice in its circulation. God's ideas are instantly available whenever I need them. Money is always available to me; I have a Divine surplus. God is my source of supply; that is my supply now; wealth of all kinds flows to me in avalanches of abundance. There is only One God and One Mind; every idea in the Mind of God is Spiritual. My relationship to money is friendly. It is a symbol of God's Wealth and His Infinite Abundance. The idea of money is omnipresent; I am one with all of the wealth in the world. I use it for good only and I thank thee, Father, for Thy supply.

Wealth Is Mine

❖

God is my source of supply, and I am one with this Infinite sup-ply. All my needs are instantaneously met at every moment of time and point of space. I demonstrate abundance now in all my affairs. I am an inlet and an outlet to the Mind of God. I am fear-less and free. I claim and feel the Spirit of prosperity. I gladly and lovingly serve my fellow man; I attract all good by an Immutable Law of attraction. There is no want, for God is the Source of all. I have instantly everything I need, since I am a Spiritual being. I am governed and supplied by God. I now bring all my empty vessels to the Infinite Storehouse within; the God-Self fills them all; there is a Divine surplus. The Divine Law responds to my faith; my faith and trust is in God, and it is well founded.

Divine Guidance

❖

All things that exist are as a ripple on the surface of the stream and all are of One Substance. All of us share in the quality of the Stream Itself, which is the mirror of myself to myself. "There is a river, the streams whereof shall make glad the city of God." I am the river of God; from me flow forth goodness, truth, and beauty. I dwell in a city of peace; this city is my own mind; all the people, which are my own thoughts, that dwell therein are God's people because they are God's Thoughts, and God's Power is with my thought of good. Infinite Intelligence is guiding me now in thought, word, and deed. I am a perfect channel of the Divine. I feel, know, and believe that my God-Self illumines my pathway. Divine Wisdom inspires, guides, governs, and directs me into all Truth. I am one with God now; all is well. I love the Voice of the Holy One within; it is the voice of my Father, and my Father is God.

How to Realize My Desire

꿰·꿱

My desire is the Voice of God speaking to me. It is the murmuring and the whispering of my heart. I know that all things are possible with God. God is my Deep-Self—the Formless, Invisible Spirit within me. Being aware of the desire, I know it must exist in the Invisible for me. I know it is mine right this moment. I accept it in my own consciousness. I know that I now have released my desire into the Creative Law, which is the Source of all creation. The Creative Law is within me; it is my own subconscious mind. I know when the idea or desire of mine is impressed in the subjective medium, it must be expressed. I know that feeling is the law, and the law is the feeling. I feel that I am now what I long to be. As I now contemplate my desire, I get the reaction which satisfies. I rejoice in the sense of possession. My whole being thrills to the reality of the fulfilled desire. I am at peace; I rejoice and give thanks, "It is done."

True Place

M y work is perfect, and I am always representing God's ideas. I am the consciousness of God; my mind is God's mind. I am the activity of God; I am expressing myself fully. I know there is a perfect law of supply and demand. I am instantly in touch with everything I need. I am in my true place now; I am giving of my talents in a wonderful way. I am Divinely compensated. My God is the Principle of all Knowledge; I know everything that I need instantly. I am one with my Father, and my Father is God. I am always reflecting the Glory, the Love, and the Activity of God. I am doing the thing I love to do. My place is with God at all times; I am one with Him now; it is so. I enter into the joy of it all. I thank you, Father, for my perfect place. All is well.

The Power to Accomplish

F or with God nothing shall be impossible." Omnipotence is within me; I am one with all the Power there is. All Truth is the Word of God. I speak the Truth; I rejoice in the Truth. I acknowledge Him; my mind is stayed on Him. I feel the Almighty Power flowing through me now, making me whole and perfect. I reflect Life; I have all power and strength. The joy of the Lord is my strength. I am now individualizing the Infinite Power of His Infinite Love. I express the inexhaustible energy of God. All is Spirit and the manifestation of Spirit. Thine, O Lord, is the Greatness, the Power, the Glory, the Victory, and the Majesty. I am strong in the Lord and in the Power of His Might. The Action of God is taking place in all my affairs; this is the Principle of Good. I know and believe that the Everlasting God in me is the Creator of the ends of the earth. He fainteth not, neither is He weary. I acknowledge this One Power; I consciously unite with It. I rejoice that I am made perfect.

Ability to Achieve

—≈·≈—

I know instantly everything I need to know, for Infinite Intelligence leads and guides me in all ways. I am the consciousness of God in action. I have absolute trust in this God-Power within me. The right ideas continually unfold in me in perfect sequence and with unfailing regularity. I am inspired from On High; I am forever mounting upward and onward. I am continually with thee. "In thy presence is fullness of joy; at thy right hand there are pleasures for evermore." I am ever joyous. I have the ability and the power to achieve. Whatever I conceive, I can give it conception. I am the activity of God, and that activity is always good. I am always passing on God's ideas to my fellowman, giving him joy and happiness. I am now expressing and manifesting the Light, which is God. I am always alert, alive, and happy. Thank you, Father!

Rising Higher

—≈·≈—

There is no fear in Love. "Perfect Love casteth out fear." I now possess a deep, inner understanding which makes me master

of all the circumstances of my life. I am in the place of dominion now. I contemplate the Divine Presence within me; I realize
His Life, Love, and Joy flow through me. There is a new buoyancy
in my step; there is a new light in my eyes. I am illumined by the
Light of the One Who Forever Is. I am abiding in Love. I am lifted
up into a higher level of consciousness; I sense the Inner Beauties and Glories of God within. Today I let Love keep me in peace
and harmony. I feel the rhythm of the universe; every atom of my
being dances to the rhythm of the Eternal God. My vision is on
Light, Love, and Truth; I am Divinely led in all ways. My eyes are
on God, and my perception is perfect now. I see God everywhere.
"Lo, I come, and I will dwell in the midst of thee, saith the Lord."

Law of Success

I am the consciousness of God in action. I know it is God working
through me, for God works by means of man. "The Law of the
Lord is perfect." There is a perfect outcome to all my activity. My
work is always successful because it is God's work, which is perfect
and divine. I have instantly everything I need because I am supplied and governed by God. I always know how to obtain everything I need. "My God shall supply all your need according to
his riches in glory." I am full of peace, harmony, and joy. I radiate
Divine Love to all mankind. I am now identified with success; I am
attracting to myself according to an Immutable Law the circumstances, conditions, ideas, finances, and all things necessary for
the unfoldment of my plans. I am Divinely led in all ways. God is
prospering me in mind, body, and affairs. I go to sleep every night
feeling successful and happy. "God giveth to his beloved in sleep."
Thank you, Father.

The Progressive Spirit

They that worship Him must worship Him in spirit and in truth." I now contemplate the fact that Infinite Intelligence dwells within me. There is a Universal Goodness, which is everywhere active and present: I am one with God, with life, the universe, and with all things. The Action of God is taking place now in all my affairs. I am prospered in mind, body, and affairs. I understand the Law of Life is one of progression; I am growing Spiritually in a wonderful way. I am in tune with the Infinite, and God is my Partner. Success is mine now, for I am identified with success and prosperity. I rejoice to see all men grow righteously. I rejoice in the success of all. The Spirit of good will flows from me to all mankind. I am full of confidence and peace. I am illumined by the Light within me. Divine Understanding is a lamp unto my feet, and underneath are the Everlasting Arms.

Eyes and Ears

I am the Lord that healeth me. My vision is spiritual, eternal, and a quality of my consciousness. My eyes are divine ideas and they are always functioning perfectly. My perception of spiritual Truth is clear and powerful. The light of understanding dawns in me; I see more and more of God's Truth every day. I see spiritually; I see mentally; I see physically. I see images of Truth and Beauty everywhere.

The Infinite Healing Presence is now, this moment, rebuilding my eyes. They are perfect, divine instruments enabling me to receive messages from the world within and the world without. The Glory of God is revealed in my eyes.

I hear the Truth; I love the Truth; I know the truth. My ears are God's perfect ideas functioning perfectly at all times. My ears are the perfect instruments which reveal God's Harmony to me. The Love, Beauty, and Harmony of God flow through my eyes and ears; I am in tune with the Infinite. I hear the Still, Small Voice of God within me. The Holy Spirit quickens my hearing, and my ears are open and free.

The Power of God

The Uplifting, Healing, Strengthening Power of the Healing Presence is now restoring every organ of my body. God in the midst of me is Mighty to heal, strengthen, purify, vitalize, and make me every whit whole.

I have complete trust in the Holy Spirit, which is the Presence of God in me. I know that this Divine Presence is bringing all my affairs into Divine order. I have "put on the new man, that after God hath created in righteousness and holiness of truth."

I see and know the Life of God is manifesting now in my flesh. I see God in my entire being; I claim that the Harmony of God is now manifesting Itself in me as strength, purity, beauty, wholeness, perfection, and eternal youth.

The rejuvenating Power of the Spirit is now operating in every cell and fiber of my being, making me whole, pure, fresh, and radiant with Divine Life and Wholeness. Every moment of my life I am growing stronger, healthier, happier, and more youthful. The Vitalizing, Tireless Energy of the Life of God is flowing through me now; I feel wonderful.

Your New Awareness

❈

The Lord is my light and my salvation; whom shall I fear? the
Lord is the strength of my life; of whom shall I be afraid?
                                        PSALMS 27:1.

Affirm daily with deep feeling: I have a new, strong conviction of God's Presence which holds me spellbound, entranced, and unmoved, and I feel serene, confident, and unafraid. I know there is nothing to fear—nothing to draw away from for God is all there is and everywhere present. In Him I live, move, and have my being; so I have no fear. God's envelope of Love surrounds me and His Golden River of Peace flows through me; all is well. I am not afraid of people, conditions, events, or circumstances for God is with me. Faith in God fills my soul, and I have no fear. I dwell in the Presence of God now and forevermore, and no fear can touch me. I am not afraid of the future for God is with me. He is my dwelling place, and I am surrounded with the whole armor of God. God created me and He sustains me. God's wisdom leads and guides me; so I cannot err. I now celebrate the New Year (conviction of God's presence) because I know in my heart the great truth, *"Closer is He than breathing, nearer than hands and feet."*

Dwelling With God

❈

I live in a state of consciousness. It is the consciousness of inner peace, joy, harmony, and good will for all men. I know that my real country is not a geographical location. A country is a dwelling place. I dwell in the Secret Place of the Most High; I abide in the Shadow of the Almighty; I walk and talk with God all the days of my life. I know there is only one Divine Family and that is humanity. *Let God arise, and his enemies be scattered.* PSALM 68:1.

I know that my only enemies are fear, ignorance, superstition, compromise, and other false gods. I will not permit these enemies to dwell in my mind. I refuse to give negative thoughts a passport to my mind.

I enthrone God and His Love in my mind. I think, feel, and act from the standpoint of Divine love. I mentally touch the Divine Power now, and It moves in my behalf; I feel invincible. Peace begins with me. I feel God's river of peace flowing through me now.

I claim the love of God permeates the hearts of all men and God and His Wisdom rule, guide, govern me and all men everywhere. God inspires me, our leaders, and the government of all nations to do His will, and His will only. The will of God is harmony, peace, joy, wholeness, beauty, and perfection. It is wonderful!

Disciplining the Mind

She was found with child of the Holy Ghost.   MATT. 1:18.

The *Holy Ghost* means the Holy (whole) Spirit or God which is lodged in the unconscious depths of all men. *Joseph* is your choosing, volitional, or conscious mind. *Mary* represents your deeper mind full of the qualities, attributes, and potencies of God. Joseph, the conscious mind, should be a guide and protector for the holy child which child is your awareness of the presence and power of God within you. Your thought is Joseph, and your feeling or emotion is Mary. When these two unite in peace and harmony, your prayer is answered; this is God in action. This is the way your mind works, and knowledge of this is the birth of the Holy Child or Wisdom in you. Practice a harmonious, synchronous, and joyous relationship between your conscious and subconscious mind and you will bring forth health, peace, strength, and security. Enthrone the right idea in your mind; then you will experience in your heart the true feeling. The union of your thought and feeling represents the married pair in you; when they are fused, the third element *peace* (God) enters in, and you experience the joy of the answered prayer. Let your heart become a chalice for God's love and a manger for His birth; as a result you will express and bring forth a child which is God on earth.

The Thankful Heart

"And one of them when he saw that he was healed, turned back, and with a loud voice glorified God. And fell down on his face at his feet giving him thanks."   LUKE 17:15, 16.

"Pray without ceasing. In every thing give thanks."
                    I THESS. 5:17, 18.

I give supreme recognition to the God-Presence within me. I sincerely and honestly give thanks for all the blessings received. I give thanks for all the good in my life; I live in the feeling of grateful rejoicing. My thankful heart strikes the magic of the divine response. Every day of my life I express thanks for my knowledge of the laws of mind and the way of the Spirit. I know that thankfulness is a movement of the heart first which is followed by a movement of the lips. My uplifted heart opens up the treasure-house of Infinity within me and bespeaks my faith in the fulfillment of my prayers. I am truly thankful because I have found God in the midst of me. "I sought the Lord, and He heard me and delivered me from all my fears." He who possesses a thankful heart is always in tune with the Infinite and cannot suppress the joy that arises from contemplating God and His Holy Presence. In everything, give thanks.

Thought Power

❧

Man is what he thinks all day long. "As a man thinketh in his heart, so is he." Have a healthy regard and a wholesome respect for your thoughts. Your health, happiness, success, and peace of mind are largely determined by your awareness of the power of thought. You have heard it said that thoughts are things, and that thoughts execute themselves. Your thought is a definite force. When you think the thought, you are actually releasing its latent power into action.

Think on whatsoever things are true, lovely, elevating, and Godlike and be absolutely convinced of the supremacy and authority of thought. You must definitely believe in your own thought, not merely as yours, but as a power in its own right; then you will make your prayers effective.

The plant is in the seed. The oak is in the acorn. You don't give the seed vitality; it has its own mathematics, mechanics, and mode of expression; likewise the thought is the power; you do not give it power. Know this and you will be free from strain and anxiety. To think with confidence in the power of your thought is the action of God in you, and "He never faileth."

Move onward and upward by recognizing the supremacy of the Spiritual Power and the authority of your thought. This is the way to get marvelous results. This knowledge augments your faith enabling you to experience the joy of the answered prayer.

Banish Anxiety

—❊·❊—

The Lord is my light and my salvation;
Whom shall I fear?
The Lord is the strength of my life;
Of whom shall I be afraid?

This one verse of the Twenty-seventh Psalm gives personal freedom from all fear. It reveals to you the source of all power, strength, and wisdom. It enables you to reject the power of externals, takes the burden off your shoulders, and sets you on the high road to peace of mind, health, and happiness.

The Lord is the Presence of God, the I AM within you. In simple, psychological language, the Lord is your consciousness. What is consciousness? Your state of consciousness is the way you think, feel, believe, and the reasoning behind your belief. The cause of all your experiences is your thought and feeling.

Refuse to give power to conditions, circumstances, and the external world. Your thought initiates causation. Your thinking is cause; the condition is not causative. There is no power to challenge Omnipotence; therefore, there is nothing to fear. If fear comes to your mind, go within to your Divine Center; think of God and His Power, realizing there is only One Power, and you are one with It now. In this stillness, nothing external can inhibit, obstruct, or thwart you. Think of new and better conditions, the way you want things to be. Realize that as you think, it is Omnipotence thinking and moving on your behalf. The outcome is sure and certain, for it is God in action.

God is the name for the One Power acting beneficently in your life. This Power is Sovereign, Supreme, One and Indivisible. It is self-moving. This Power inspires you, guides you, watches over you, strengthens you, and protects you in ways you know not of. God lives and reigns in your life. A realization of this truth is your salvation.

A Better Future

ᐊᔓᐅ

God hath not given us the spirit of fear, but
of power, and of love, and of a sound mind.

Each day is a time of renewal, resurgence, and rebirth. All nature proclaims the glory of a new day. This is to remind us that we must awaken the God within us and arise from our long winter sleep of limitation and walk forth into the morning of a new day and a new life. Fear, ignorance, and superstition must die in us, and we must resurrect faith, confidence, love, and good will.

Begin now to take the following transfusion of God's grace and love, "I am filled with the freeflowing, cleansing, healing, harmonizing, vitalizing life of the Holy Spirit. My body is the temple of the Living God, and it is pure, whole, and perfect in every part.

Every function of my mind and body is controlled and governed by Divine Wisdom and Divine Order.

I now look forward to a glorious future. I live in the joyous expectancy of the best. All the wonderful God-like thoughts I am thinking now, this day, sink down into the subconscious mind as into a tomb. I know when their time is ready, they will come forth as harmony, health, peace, conditions, experiences, and events.

I now pass over from fear and lack to freedom in God and the abundant life. The God-man is risen in me. Behold! I make all things new!"

The Holy Man
(Adapted from The Holy Shadow)

Long, long ago, there lived a Holy Man so good that the astonished angels came from heaven to see how one could be so godly. He simply went about his daily life radiating love as the star diffuses light and the flowers perfume without even being aware of it. Two words summed up his day: He gave, and he forgave. Yet these words never fell from his lips; they were expressed in his ready smile, his kindness, love, and good will.

The angels said to God, "Oh Lord, grant him the gift of miracles!"

God replied, "I consent; ask what he wishes."

"What do you desire then?" cried the angels.

"What can I wish for?" asked the Holy Man smiling. "That God give me His grace, with that should I not have everything?"

The angels insisted, "You must ask for a miracle, or one will be forced upon you."

"Very well," said the Holy Man, "that I may do a great deal of good without ever knowing it."

The angels were greatly perplexed. They took counsel together and resolved upon the following plan: Every time the Holy Man's shadow should fall behind him, or at either side, so that he could not see it, it should have the power to cure disease, soothe pain, and comfort sorrow.

And so it came to pass. When the Holy Man walked along, his shadow on the ground, on either side or behind him, made arid paths green, caused withered plants to bloom, gave clear water to dried-up brooks, fresh color to pale little children, and joy to unhappy mothers. The Holy Man simply went about his daily life pouring forth love as the star diffuses light and the flower perfume without ever being aware of it.

And the people respecting his humility followed him silently, never speaking about his miracles. Little by little, they came even to forget his name, and called him only, "The Holy Man."

Discovering the Power

You will discover the deep reservoirs of power the moment you assume they are there and act as though you were convinced of that great truth. "He who perseveres to the end shall be saved."

Success, the answer to your prayer, the solution you are seeking come as you keep on keeping on. You never give up; neither do you take "No" for an answer. Keep on moving forward. The athlete who is running in a race ofttimes gets tired, weary, exhausted, and ready to give up. He rejects the thought of failure completely by calling on the God-Power to renew his strength;

then a tremendous change takes place. A great wave of strength and vitality moves through him. The psychologist calls it his "second wind."

Don't stop before you get your second wind or you will never discover the Hidden Power. The Power that moves the world is within you. Act as though you believed it is there and you will work miracles in your life, transcending your wildest dreams.

"But they that wait upon the Lord shall renew their strength; they shall mount up with wings as eagles; they shall run, and not be weary; and they shall walk, and not faint." ISA. 40:31.

Let Go and Let God Do It

❧

You have been given dominion. You are the master of your thoughts, emotions, and responses to life. Your thought is creative, because your subconscious mind responds to the nature of your thought. When you pray, you must be a very good executive; you must learn to delegate your work wisely and judiciously. God in His Wisdom has given you a subconscious mind which is a wonderful servant. It obeys your command. You are the captain decreeing orders, and your subconscious mind faithfully carries out your decrees. When you have a problem, you turn your request for a solution over to the Deeper Mind which is in touch with Infinite Intelligence and Boundless Wisdom. The Deeper Mind knows how to solve your problem and present you with the answer. Turn your request over now with faith and confidence knowing in your heart you will have actually turned your request over or not by the way you feel inside. If you trust the inner power, you are peaceful and calm. *In quietness and confidence shall be your strength.* Isaiah 30:15.

Words of Power

✣

I stay my mind upon God and I am kept in perfect peace. In this peace of God I find Order, Harmony, and Divine Love.

"No word of God shall be void of power."

The words that I speak are full of spirit and full of life. I acknowledge God in all my affairs and transactions. My mind is stayed on Him. I am blessed and prospered by the activity of the law of good operating in my life.

All my statements of truth are charged with life, love, and meaning. The words I speak make a deep impression on my deeper mind. I am glad I know God dwells in my heart, for God is the very life of me. These words sink into my heart, "Behold, I dwell with thee, O man of God, and thou dwellest with me."

I know that when I look at my fellow man, I am seeing God in human form. I bless and send forth loving thoughts to all mankind. I speak the word now. My words are creative; the deeper mind within me responds. I now decree perfect health, harmony, and peace in my home, my heart, and all my affairs.

I know and believe that God is guiding me now in all my ways, and that Infinite Spirit governs all my actions. I have decreed it; it shall come to pass. I have found the Jewel of Eternity in my own heart.

Prosperity

❧·❧

Let the words of my mouth, and the meditation of my heart, be
acceptable in thy sight, O Lord, my strength, and my redeemer.
PSALM 19:14.

One of the best ways to bring prosperity into your life is to have the thankful heart. Always give thanks, and praise the increase which comes to you.

If you select a rose bush in your garden, and bless it several times a day, it will respond with a lavish blossoming which will exceed all the other roses.

Give thanks by having the grateful and uplifted heart for the wonderful food on the table. You prosper by blessing members of the household and all people everywhere. To bless the other, claim that the Presence of God is in the person, and that he is radiating and expressing more and more of God's Love, Light, and Truth. Bless all of your relatives; bless every situation; bless your home, your environment, your work, and your office. You are actually putting into application one of the great laws of prosperity also.

To prosper means to grow spiritually, mentally, and materially. Claim now: "I am going to put the law of prosperity into operation in a wonderful way in my life!" Do it in this way: Say frequently, "I bless and prosper every member of my family. I give thanks, I praise, and I exalt God in my husband, my wife, and in my children. I bless everything they are doing. I bless all of the gifts I make. I know it is more blessed to give than to receive. I bless my business. I pray for and bless my workers, my customers, and all people. My work prospers, multiplies, increases, and returns to me a thousand fold."

Onward and Upward

Maintain a positive, constructive attitude of mind and you will move onward, upward, and Godward. Sometimes people will tell you about the bad things that are bound to come; it seems that they do not know any reason why something good should happen. They say prayer is a state of wishful thinking. *Wishful thinking* to them means a wish that cannot be realized, or a wish that is too good to be true.

There is not anything too good to be true nor is there anything too wonderful to last. Claim your good now and walk in the assumption that all good things are yours.

Desires knock at the door of every heart. It is the inner voice within all of us which is saying, "Come on up higher!" Prayer is entering into the realization of the wish fulfilled. If wishful thinking is wishing or desiring something without realizing it, let us ask who is the wishful thinker? He is the person who does not understand prayer. He desires health, wealth, prosperity, and true expression, but he says in his heart, "I do not believe; I have no faith." In other words he lacks faith and confidence to which the everlasting principle of life responds in all of us.

The scientific thinker knows there is a way to realize an answer to his desires. He recognizes there is a subjective law within him which responds to his faith and conviction. He realizes if he prays believing, he shall receive. His faith is well founded; he is at peace. Such a person has turned his request over to this other mind knowing it will answer him.

Do not look at the top of the mountain and say, "It is impossible!" You are in Truth. Your vision is on the Summit, and your faith will take you there.

God's Circle of Love

The gifts of God are mine now. I live in the Presence of God from whom all blessings flow. I use every moment of this day to glorify God. God's harmony, peace, and abundance are mine now. Divine love flowing from me blesses all who come into my atmosphere. God's love is felt by all present here, and His love is healing them now.

I fear no evil for God is with me. I am always surrounded by the sacred circle of God's love and power. I claim, feel, know, and believe definitely and positively that the spell of God's love and eternal watchfulness guides, heals, and watches over me and all members of my family.

I forgive everyone, and I sincerely radiate God's love, peace and good will to all men everywhere. At the center of my being is peace; this is the peace of God. In this stillness I feel His strength, guidance, and the love of His Holy Presence. I am divinely guided in all my ways. I am a clear channel for God's love, light, truth, and beauty. I feel His River of Peace flowing through me now. I know that all my problems are dissolved in the mind of God. God's ways are my ways. The words I have spoken accomplish that whereunto they are sent. I rejoice and give thanks realizing my prayers are answered. It is so.

How to Give a Treatment

Spiritual treatment means that you turn to the Indwelling God and remind yourself of His peace, harmony, wholeness, beauty, boundless love, and limitless Power. Know that God loves you and cares for you. As you pray this way the fear will gradually fade away. If you pray for a heart condition, do not think of the organ as diseased as this would not be spiritual thinking. Thoughts are things. Your spiritual thought takes the form of cells, tissues, nerves, and organs. To think of a damaged heart or high blood pressure tends to suggest more of what you already have. Cease dwelling on symptoms, organs, or any part of the body. Turn your mind to God and His love. Feel and know that there is only one healing Presence and Power, and to its corollary: *There is no power to challenge the action of God.*

—o—

Quietly and lovingly affirm that the uplifting, healing, strengthening Power of the healing Presence is flowing through you making you every whit whole. Know and feel that the harmony, beauty, and Life of God manifest in you as strength, peace, vitality, beauty, wholeness, and right action. Get a clear realization of this, and the damaged heart or other diseased condition will dissolve in the Light of God's love.

Glorify God in your Body. I COR. 6:20.

About the Author

A native of Ireland who resettled in America, Joseph Murphy, Ph.D., D.D. (1898–1981) was a prolific and widely admired New Thought minister and writer, best known for his metaphysical classic, *The Power of Your Subconscious Mind*, an international bestseller since it first appeared on the self-help scene in 1963. A popular speaker, Murphy lectured on both American coasts and in Europe, Asia, and South Africa. His many books and pamphlets on the auto-suggestive and metaphysical faculties of the human mind have entered multiple editions—some of the most poignant of which appear in this volume. Murphy is considered one of the pioneering voices of affirmative-thinking philosophy.

Printed in the USA
CPSIA information can be obtained
at www.ICGtesting.com
JSHW051023230524
R13534700005B/R135347PG63569JSX00009B/5